Macromedia®
Dreamweaver® MX
KillerTips

The hottest collection of cool tips and hidden secrets for Macromedia® Dreamweaver® MX

MACROMEDIA DREAMWEAVER MX

TIPS

Joseph Lowery
Angela C. Buraglia

Killer Tips series developed by Scott Kelby

PUBLISHER
David Dwyer

ASSOCIATE PUBLISHER
Stephanie Wall

PRODUCTION MANAGER
Gina Kanouse

SENIOR ACQUISITIONS EDITOR
Linda Anne Bump

SENIOR MARKETING MANAGER
Tammy Detrich

PUBLICITY MANAGER
Susan Nixon

COPY EDITOR
Kathy Murray

INDEXER
Lisa Stumpf

COMPOSITION
Wil Cruz

MANUFACTURING COORDINATOR
Dan Uhrig

COVER DESIGN AND
CREATIVE CONCEPTS
Felix Nelson

www.newriders.com
www.dwkillertips.com

Copyright © 2003 by New Riders Publishing

International Standard Book Number: 0-7357-1302-2

Library of Congress Catalog Card Number: 2002101877

Printed in the United States of America

First edition: January 2003

07 06 05 04 03   7 6 5 4 3 2

Interpretation of the printing code: The rightmost double-digit number is the year of the book's printing; the rightmost single-digit number is the number of the book's printing. For example, the printing code 03-1 shows that the first printing of the book occurred in 2003.

Trademarks

Warning and Disclaimer

This one's for all the killer designers and developers who have pushed the

envelope all the way to the mailbox—and delivered!

—JOSEPH LOWERY

For my son, Gaetano, with all my love.

—ANGELA C. BURAGLIA

ACKNOWLEDGMENTS

A special tip o' the hat to the hardest-working team in the Killer Tip biz: Derren, Jay, Lisa, Zac, and especially Angela. We've had a great time putting these tips together and it's been a blast working together. I really appreciate the seriously hard effort put into the work by all concerned. Thanks also to the folks at New Riders: Linda, Gina, Steve, David, Chris, and all the rest. And, of course, we wouldn't be anywhere without the beauty of an idea from Scott Kelby—thanks for the lead, Scott.

—*JOSEPH LOWERY*

. . . .

If it were not for the help and encouragement of Wojciech Miskiewicz in my earliest days with Dreamweaver, I'd probably have given up and found another career. Thank you Wojciech! Daniel Short, Massimo Foti, Danilo Celic, Brad Halstead, Ray West, Paul R. Boon, Murray R. Summers, Trent Pastrana, Eddie Traversa, and Jay A. Grantham, you've helped and inspired me more than you'll ever know and I am eternally thankful. There are too many DreamweaverFAQ.com tutorial authors to name you all, but I do want you to know I appreciate each and every one of you. Marcello Cerruti, Laurie Casolino, Alex Mariño and Bryan Ashcraft: When I was helping you on MSN chat, you were really helping me, so I thank you; our MSN chats helped inspire many of the tips found in this book.

Thanks to my co-author, Joseph Lowery, for choosing me to write this book with him. Joe is an incredible inspiration not only to me, but also to many Dreamweaver fans worldwide. His sense of humor and ability to stay positive through stressful times has been a very positive influence on me. He's an absolute pleasure to work with, and I've learned so much from him. He even let me take up most of the acknowledgements space!

I also want to thank Derren Whiteman and Jay A. Grantham for taking all the great screenshots in this book. They really pulled through for us and got the job done. Without the watchful eyes of Lisa Boesen, Zac VanNote, and Stephanie Sullivan, this book wouldn't be the same. Special thanks to Kathy Murray for making me sound smarter! It is always a pleasure working with the New Riders team.

To my wonderful husband, Ambrogio, thank you for your incredible patience, understanding, and for taking care of our adorable little Gaetano as I work on all my projects. I love you, honey! Mom and Dad, if it weren't for your constant help and support I don't know what I'd do or where I'd be. Thank you for everything.

—*ANGELA C. BURAGLIA*

ABOUT THE AUTHORS

Joseph Lowery is the author of *Joseph Lowery's Beyond Dreamweaver* and the co-author of a forthcoming book tentatively titled *Macromedia Dreamweaver Web Application Recipies* (New Riders) as well as the *Dreamweaver MX Bible* and the *Fireworks MX Bible* series (both Wiley). His books are international best-sellers, having sold over 300,000 copies world-wide in nine different languages. As a programmer, Joseph contributed two extensions to the latest release of Fireworks MX. He is also a consultant and trainer and has presented at Seybold in both Boston and San Francisco, Macromedia UCON in the U.S. and Europe, ThunderLizard's Web World, and other locations around the globe—ranging from New Zealand to Las Vegas. As a partner in Deva Associates, Ltd., Joseph developed the Deva Tools for Dreamweaver set of navigational extensions.

. . . .

Angela C. Buraglia is the founder of DreamweaverFAQ.com, but she came to the web development profession in a round-about manner. Angela realized she wanted a career that would allow her to start a family and stay home with her husband and child. In an effort to give back to the Macromedia Dreamweaver newsgroup community that helped and encouraged her in her new career, she founded DreamweaverFAQ.com. Although she only intended to be a web developer, life's path has led her to become that and more. In addition to her contribution to this book, Angela was a contributing author to *Dreamweaver MX Magic* (New Riders), a contributing author to *The ColdFusion MX Web Application Construction Kit* (Macromedia Press), the lead technical editor for the *Dreamweaver MX Bible* (Wiley Publishing, formerly Hungry Minds), and involved in one way or another with several other Dreamweaver-related books. Currently, she is also a Team Macromedia volunteer for Dreamweaver.

Angela's future plans are to continue developing DreamweaverFAQ.com, to build and sell Dreamweaver extensions, to give presentations at conferences, and perhaps to become involved in new book projects. Long gone are the days of applying makeup; now Angela applies behaviors and CSS to web sites— and most importantly—is home with her little boy.

Angela lives in Brea, California, with her husband, Ambrogio, and 2-year-old son, Gaetano.

These reviewers contributed their considerable hands-on expertise to the entire development process for *Dreamweaver MX Killer Tips*. As the book was being written, these dedicated professionals reviewed all the material for technical content, organization, and flow. Their feedback was critical to ensuring that *Dreamweaver Killer Tips* fits our reader's need for the highest-quality technical information.

Lisa Boesen is a technical writer who specializes in designing, writing, and implementing online documentation in various formats, including HTML, Adobe Acrobat, and HTML Help. Lisa paid her dues by spending many years as a systems programmer, writing assembly language code for a complex operating system. Her background in computer science, her experience as a software developer, and her empathy for the end user prepared her for her career shift to technical writing. Most recently, she was a contributing author for the *Dreamweaver MX Bible* (Wiley).

Zac Van Note, who recently contributed a project to *Dreamweaver MX Magic* (New Riders), earned a BFA degree in graphic design at New Mexico State University. He's written, drawn, and published comic books. As a graphic designer, he's created numerous catalogs and web sites. Since 1998, Zac has taught dozens of classes at the University of New Mexico, including Photoshop, QuarkXPress, and Dreamweaver. He was recently recognized with an Outstanding Instructor award at UNM. The site he created for his students, www.design-link.org, is a good reference for anyone interested in computer graphics.

Stephanie Sullivan owns VioletSky Design (http://www.violetsky.net) in coastal North Carolina where she creates sublime, fast-loading websites for businesses and creatives. She has recently taken on writing and technical editing. You will find her glued to her Dual G4 about 12 hours a day madly keeping up with her clients, taking care of her husband and two boys, participating in several web design forums, and talking to the little people that live inside her computer. In her spare time, her hobbies are creating websites and studying web development.

ABOUT THE TECHNICAL ASSISTANTS

These contributors lent their expertise to the creation of *Dreamweaver MX Killer Tips* by creating the illustrative screen captures that accompany each of the tips. Their dedication and hard work has helped to ensure the quality and usefulness of each of the tips.

Jay A. Grantham is the owner, developer, chief cook, and bottle washer of *WebsiteIC* web development. He is a contributing author to the Dreamweaver reference site dwfaq.com, a member of the International Webmasters Association and has done peer reviews for many authors. He enjoys learning what Dreamweaver can do for him and what he can do for the Dreamweaver community. Jay lives in Houston, Texas with is wife/best friend, Dana, and their two small children, Garrett and Katelyn. When he is not online, he is most likely fighting fires and saving lives as a member of the Houston Fire Department.

Derren Whiteman began building web sites by hand and later took up Dreamweaver after joining Mediafear, a San Francisco web design shop where he spent three years building web sites. Derren has also served as an Information Technology consultant and computer instructor. He spends much of his time in technical publishing. He co-wrote the *Fireworks MX Bible* (Wiley), served as technical editor for versions 3 and 4 of the *Fireworks Bible* and *Dreamweaver 4 Bible* (Wiley), and has numerous other titles under his belt. Derren is a Macromedia Certified Dreamweaver Developer and maintains a number of web sites, including FrancinePaul.com, Konis.com, and Derren.com. He makes his home in Toronto, Ontario, Canada.

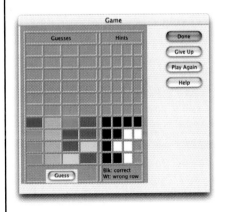

TABLE OF CONTENTS

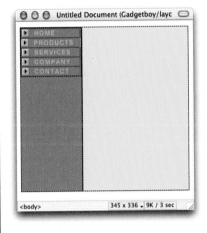

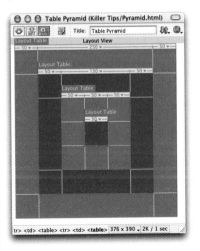

TABLE OF CONTENTS

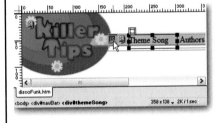

TABLE OF CONTENTS

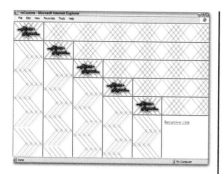

Rev Your Engines
Templates, Library, and Production Tips

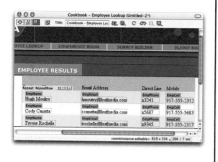

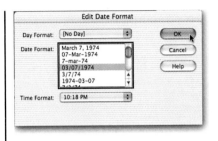

CHAPTER 7   133
Maximum Acceleration
Dreamweaver Tip Variety Pack

TABLE OF CONTENTS

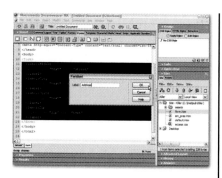

TABLE OF CONTENTS

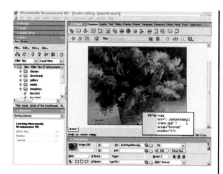

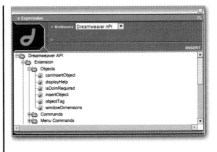

TELL US WHAT YOU THINK

As the reader of this book, you are the most important critic and commentator. We value your opinion and want to know what we're doing right, what we could do better, what areas you'd like to see us publish in, and any other words of wisdom you're willing to pass our way.

As the Senior Acquisitions Editor on this book, I welcome your comments. You can fax, email, or write me directly to let me know what you did or didn't like about this book—as well as what we can do to make our books stronger. When you write, please be sure to include this book's title, ISBN, and author, as well as your name and phone or fax number. I will carefully review your comments and share them with the author and editors who worked on the book.

Please note that I cannot help you with technical problems related to the topic of this book, and that due to the high volume of email I receive, I might not be able to reply to every message.

Fax: 317-581-4663

Email: linda.bump@newriders.com

Mail: Linda Bump
          Senior Acquisitions Editor
          New Riders Publishing
          201 West 103rd Street
          Indianapolis, IN 46290 USA

INTRODUCTION

Why we wrote this book

Sitting around the virtual café one day, we had a great idea.

"Hey, we know some stuff," we said to each other, "Maybe the stuff we know could help other folks interested in the same stuff."

"Yeah, but, it's got to be the best stuff, the crème de la crème stuff, the greatest stuff on earth!" we agreed.

"Killer Stuff!" we exclaimed simultaneously.

After several Internet-years of research ('bout a week-and-a-half in so-called "real time"), we realized what we had wasn't just a bunch of stuff; it was a full range of time-saving, productivity-enhancing, Dreamweaver MX tips with an energy efficiency rating of 11.3. You've seen tips like these before, sprinkled through every major Dreamweaver book ever published (and there have been a few), appearing in sidebars or as special asides, typically with cutesy icons created as an exercise in Design 101. Quite often, those tips, notes, and warnings are what really super-charge a book, inspiring "Aha!s," "Oh, Now I get it!s," and "Why didn't they tell me this earlier?s" all across the land.

So what makes this book special? Let us count the ways. First, we've dispensed with everything but the tips! You won't have to wade through pages and pages of overviews or feature descriptions to get to the good stuff. Second, we've obliterated all those annoying little icons—just blew 'em to smithereens! They blew up real good.* Third, there's one thing the tips in all those regular Dreamweaver books don't have that we have in abundance: pictures! Full-color figures illustrate nearly every tip—it's the closest thing to a mind meld this side of Vulcan.*

Is this book for you?

What's that you say—you just need to know one more thing and you'll reach perfect Dreamweaver enlightenment? Then, yes, this is the book for you! This is a book filled with the things you need to know to get the most out of Dreamweaver and use it to build blindingly sharp, cutting-edge websites. All you need to get going with this book is a rudimentary working knowledge of Dreamweaver—if you can perform the basic operations and know your way around the interface, you're good to go.

Remember the Incredible Shrinking Man? Well, Dreamweaver is the Incredible Growing Program, gaining complexity and power with every release—and *Dreamweaver MX Killer Tips* is your guidebook to all the shortcuts and secret treasures buried there.

Inside jokes—If you don't get 'em, just give a little knowing snort and a minor smirk and nobody will know.

Okay, how do I get started?

Take a handkerchief or scarf and fold it a couple of times so that it is about three inches wide and opaque. Wrap it around your eyes and tie it at the back of your head like a blindfold. Hold the book in one hand, and flip through the pages with the other hand. At a random moment, stab your finger some place on one of the pages. Keep your finger where it is and remove the blindfold (this may take some rubbing of your head up against a wall). Read the tip your finger is pointing out. Presto—instant knowledge. Repeat about 300 times. Okay, you can just close your eyes instead of using the blindfold, but you'll have much less to talk about if your mother should happen to walk in the room while you're doing this.

The point is (no, not the finger again) that you can start anywhere and read the tips in any order. Although most of the chapters are based on a particular theme, such as CSS or extensibility, the tips themselves are self-contained and don't follow any particular sequence. This means that if you're doing a site using a lot of Templates and Library Items, you might want to focus on Chapter 6, "*Rev Your Engines:* Templates, Library, and Production Tips" Or, you can skim a number of chapters at a time in a personal test of high-geek knowledge. But don't even think about curling up with this book on the sofa—there are way too many good ideas here for you to drift off to sleep.

Is this book for Macintosh, Windows, or both?

Yes.

Flip through the book quickly—go on, we'll wait. Notice that about half the pictures are from Macintosh and half from Windows? We know there are Dreamweaver users on both sides of the fence and we want everyone to feel at home. The two interfaces are close to identical and also represent the different options available in Dreamweaver MX. Where there are differences—mostly in the keyboard shortcuts—we present both options, typically with Windows first and the Macintosh equivalent in parentheses. Hey, what can I tell you? Bill and Steve tossed a coin—a gold Krugerrand, I think, valued at your net worth— and Bill won.

Is there a website?

Dreamweaver MX Killer Tips not only has a website, but we're also closing the deal on a reality series for Fox called "Tips!" The theme song goes like this, "Good tips, good tips, what 'cha gonna do? What 'cha gonna do when they read through you?" But, until that airs, you'll just have to visit the site at www.dwkillertips.com to uncover the latest wave of super-cool tips or if you want, contact the authors to offer us fabulously high-paying jobs with little or no real work involved.

So what are you waiting for? Power up that copy of Dreamweaver MX and prepare to hit the afterburner switch with *Dreamweaver MX Killer Tips*.

Dreamweaver MX Killer Tips
Edited by Scott Kelby

Welcome to *Dreamweaver MX Killer Tips*. As Editor for the Killer Tips series, I can't tell you how excited and truly gratified I am to see this concept of creating a book that is cover-to-cover nothing but tips, extend from my original book (*Photoshop Killer Tips*) into *Dreamweaver MX Killer Tips*.

The idea for this series of books came to me when I was at the bookstore looking through the latest Photoshop books on the shelf. I found myself doing the same thing to every book I picked up: I'd turn the page until I found a paragraph that started with the word "Tip." I'd read the tip, then I'd keep turning until I found another sidebar tip. I soon realized I was hooked on tips, because I knew that if I were writing the book that's where I'd put all my best material. Think about it: If you were writing a book, and you had a really cool tip, an amazing trick, or an inside secret or shortcut, you wouldn't bury it among hundreds of paragraphs of text. No way! You'd make it stand out: You'd put a box around it, maybe put a tint behind it, and if it was really cool (and short and sweet), you'd get everybody's attention by starting with the word "Tip!"

That's what got me thinking. Obviously, I'm not the only one who likes these tips, because almost every software book has them. There's only one problem: There's never *enough* of them. And I thought, "Wouldn't it be great if there were a book that was nothing but those cool little tips?" (Of course, the book wouldn't actually have sidebars, since what's in the sidebars would be the focus: nothing but cool shortcuts, inside secrets, slick ways to do the things we do everyday, but faster—and more fun—than ever!) That was the book I really wanted, and thanks to the wonderful people at New Riders, that's the book they let me write (along with my co-author and good friend Felix Nelson). It was called *Photoshop Killer Tips*, and it became an instant bestseller because Felix and I were committed to creating something special: A book where every page included yet another tip that would make you nod your head, smile, and think "Ahhh, so that's how they do it."

TIP

If you were writing a book, and you had a really cool tip, an amazing trick, or an inside secret or shortcut, you wouldn't bury it among hundreds of paragraphs of text. You'd make it stand out: You'd put a box around it, maybe put a tint behind it, and if it was really cool (and short and sweet), you'd get everybody's attention by starting with the word "Tip!"

If you've ever wondered how the pros get twice the work done in half the time, it's really no secret: They do everything as efficiently as possible. They don't do *anything* the hard way. They know every timesaving short-cut, every workaround, every speed tip, and as such they work at full speed all the time. They'll tell you, when it comes to being efficient, and when it comes to staying ahead of the competition: Speed Kills!

Well, what you're holding in your hand is another Killer Tips book: A book packed cover-to-cover with nothing but those cool little sidebar tips (without the sidebars) and Joseph Lowery and Angela Buraglia have really captured the spirit and flavor of what a Killer Tips book is all about. I can't wait for you to get into it, so I'll step aside and let them take the wheel, because you're about to get faster, more efficient, and have more fun in Dreamweaver MX than you ever thought possible.

Have fun and enjoy the ride!

All my best,

Scott Kelby, Series Editor

"We're here at the first public tryouts for that just-announced Olympic event, web development, speaking with the sport's rising star, Webifyin' Jones. Tell me, Webifyin', what gives you your edge?"

Built For Speed
dreamweaver interface tips

"It's all in the machine, Pat, all in the machine. I'm just there to guide it."

"And guide it you do. So, tell me about your tool, then. What do you have under the hood?"

"It's Dreamweaver MX, Pat. Straight out of the box."

"I don't know about that, Webifyin'. Looks like you did a fair bit of customization on that puppy."

"That's the beauty of it, Pat. I can shape Dreamweaver to work the way I want to work and really max out its performance. Whether I'm laying it down in Design mode or cruising in Code view, Dreamweaver helps me give the best that I've got."

"I notice you seem to have sort of a manual you're clutching. Is that your secret weapon?"

"I'm sorry, but I can't reveal all my sources, Pat. I will say, however, that the first chapter of this book is really a killer when it comes to squeezing the most performance out of Dreamweaver's workspace. It's got more tips on working with panels, toolbars, and shortcuts than I ever thought possible. Just thinking about it gets my engines revving."

"Alright, Webifyin', here come the judges— you go for the gold!"

ARRANGING PANELS IN THE MX WORKSPACE

I really don't see what the big deal is about the option for changing from the Dreamweaver MX workspace to the HomeSite/Coder style workspace (Windows only). Let's compare them for a moment: HomeSite Coder opens in Code view and has panels grouped on the left. The default MX workspace has the panels grouped on the right. Aside from that, there are a few other minor differences, but in reality they're very much the same thing. In fact, despite the chosen workspace, I can drag my panel groups and dock them on the left or right sides of the Document window. Naturally, I can choose the document view (Code, Design, or Code and Design). So where's the difference? I'm telling you that there really is none! The workspace dialog is just a Dreamweaver Preference setting that is intended as a workspace starting point that you will customize to your liking as time goes on.

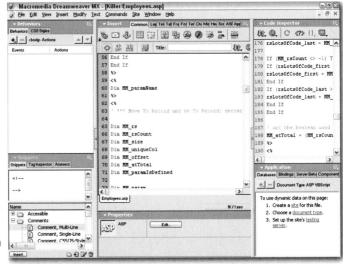

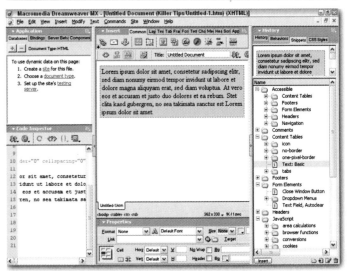

To dock a Panel group, click and drag the Panel group by its gripper and release it when the Panel group is in position (Windows and the Mac). Centered on the divider between the Panel groups and the document area is an expand/collapse arrow that collapses the width/height of the Panel groups or returns them to their previous state (Windows only). Check out the illustrations; I bet you can't tell which workspace they started as originally!

CODE INSPECTOR: TOP, BOTTOM, RIGHT, OR LEFT?

In the Dreamweaver MX or Coder Style workspace, the Code inspector (Window > Others > Code Inspector or F10) can only be docked above or below the Document window. You simply cannot dock the Code inspector to the right or left of the Document window—but we have ways. Here's

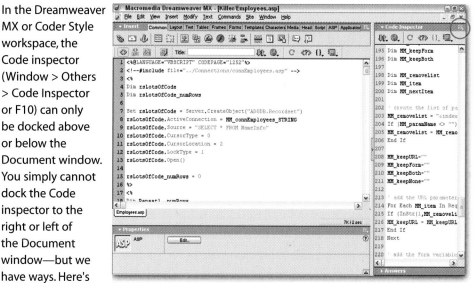

how you can outsmart Dreamweaver: Use the Options menu to select Group Code Inspector with *Whatever*—where *Whatever* is another Panel group that is already on the left or right of the workspace. I use the Answers panel to do this because by default it is not grouped with other panels.

If you want the Code inspector to be all by itself, select the other panel in the group and then choose Group Answers with New Panel Group from the Options menu. The Answers panel breaks free and floats, leaving the Code inspector where it was. With the Code inspector docked on the left or right, and the Document window in Code view, you have the benefit of what I like to call Code-Code view—which is similar to a popular Macromedia HomeSite feature.

   ## NEXT DOCUMENT, PLEASE

Moving from document to document doesn't require that you use your mouse. Similar to the way you can Alt+Tab (Option+Tab) between different programs or windows, Dreamweaver offers a shortcut for moving between open documents: Ctrl+Tab. (Mac users: this tip will not work in OS9.) Use this shortcut whenever you have a Document window in focus and want the next document in line to be brought to the front.

   LOST FLOATING PANELS—CASH REWARD

If you've ever lost your floating panels, you know just how irritating and frustrating it can be. This is less likely to happen now using the MX workspace (Windows only) than it was in the Dreamweaver 4 or Macintosh workspace. In fact, Macromedia must have thought it entirely impossible to drag a panel off screen in the MX workspace because the Window > Arrange Panels option is grayed out in the menu for this workspace. If you're using the Dreamweaver 4 or Macintosh workspace, use the Window > Arrange Panels option to snap your floating panels back onscreen in an arrangement similar to the default panel positions.

If you're using the MX workspace, that option is unavailable, so your only choice is to uninstall Dreamweaver and then reinstall it. Just kidding! You don't have to go to those lengths just to get your panels back. What you can do is change to the Dreamweaver 4 workspace using the Change Workspace button in the General category of Preferences.

You need to close and restart Dreamweaver to initiate the workspace change. Then go back into Edit > Preferences or Ctrl+U and change your workspace back to the MX workspace of your choice. Restart Dreamweaver once again, and you'll find all your panels restored to their default positions. That sure beats uninstall/reinstall, doesn't it? If you don't want to lose your custom layout, you could try changing your screen resolution and then drag the panel to the center of the screen before changing resolution again.

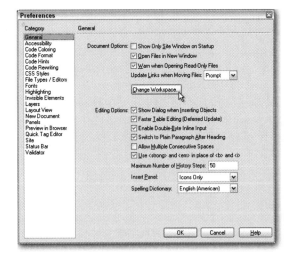

   ## EXPANDING THE PROPERTY INSPECTOR

Located in the lower-right corner of the Property inspector is a tiny little expander arrow that toggles its height. The most commonly used options are all in the top half of the Property inspector, with the less-often used options in the lower half. There really is no need to use that tiny little arrow to expand or collapse the height of the Property inspector; you can double-click on any portion of the panel (not the Panel group title bar) not occupied by an icon, field, or button.

If you're not using the Property inspector and want to regain some vertical workspace, you can hide or redisplay the Property inspector using the Ctrl+F3 (Command+F3) keyboard shortcut or by selecting Window > Properties.

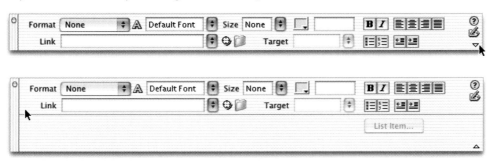

  ## CONTEXT MENUS

Context menus are all over the place in the Dreamweaver environment, often in places you may not think to try. With few exceptions, panels have at least one context menu. Typical commands, such as Copy and Paste, are usually found in a context menu, as well as other commands that relate to the item in focus at the time you right-click (Ctrl+click) to display the context menu. There are even some commands found in context menus not found else-where in the interface. The moral of the story is this: look for context menus everywhere you can in Dreamweaver and get familiar with your options. Knowing the easiest and quickest way to do things will really help improve your workflow. The fewer the clicks it takes to do something, the more efficient you'll be in your Dreamweaver development.

 PANEL ICONS & LAUNCHER

If you prefer icons or buttons to
menus and keyboard shortcuts,
you'll want to enable the
Launcher. Select Edit >
Preferences (Dreamweaver >
Preferences on Mac OS X) or
Ctrl+U (Command+U) and then
choose Panels in the category
list on the left. Click the checkbox to enable icons in panels
and the Launcher. Use the Add
(+) button to choose more
panels to have shown by their
respective icon in the launcher
or select a panel in the current

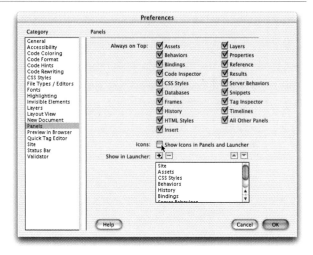

list and click the Remove (–) button to exclude panels. When you are satisfied with your
selections, click OK. Dreamweaver now displays an icon to the left of the panel name in each
panel's tab. In the lower right of the Document window, the Launcher is shown with icons
for each panel specified in your preferences. Clicking an icon will show its respective panel if
the panel is not already visible and will hide the panel if it is currently visible.

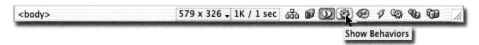

Show Behaviors

 LOCATING FILES

Dreamweaver conveniently displays the folder name and
filename in the title bar of open documents. Because it is
possible that you could have multiple folders within your
site that have the same name, seeing only one folder level
in the path to the file in the title bar isn't always enough.
No more digging through each folder trying to find where
the current file belongs; Site > Locate in Site, will find the
current document in the Site panel and select it for you.

8   **CHAPTER 1** • Dreamweaver Interface Tips

PEEK-A-BOO PANELS

Let's face it; panels take up a lot of valuable horizontal and vertical space. Sometimes when you're working on a layout in Design view, you really need to see the full picture. This is one keyboard shortcut I advise you to learn: F4. Press that F4 key whenever you want to rid your workspace of all panels; then press F4 to bring them all back again. If you're the menu-using type, you'll find Window > Hide Panels or Window > Show Panels just as useful. If you're working in the Dreamweaver 4 or Macintosh workspace, you'll need to maximize your Document window. If you're working in the Dreamweaver MX workspace, however, you'll need to maximize your document only if it wasn't already maximized when you pressed F4.

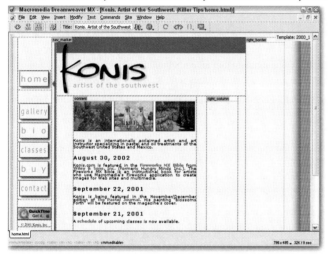 

   STANDARD TOOLBAR

Sometimes the simplest of features can please the masses and this is certainly in that category. The Standard toolbar offers—at the touch of a button—the typical commands you'd find in most any program: New Document, Open, Save, Save All, Cut, Copy, Paste, Undo, and Redo. The same commands found on the Standard toolbar are also located in either the File or Edit menu, but sometimes it is just easier to press a button. By default, the Standard toolbar is turned off. You can display this toolbar two ways: Select View > Toolbars > Standard or right-click (Ctrl+click) the Document toolbar in an area that is free of buttons or fields and choose Standard from the context menu.

WHAT'S YOUR ORIENTATION?

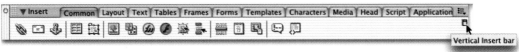

Mac users may not have a choice of workspaces like Windows users do; however, Mac users have at least one option that is not available in the Windows workspace. Remember the Objects panel from Dreamweaver 4 (since renamed the Insert bar as of Dreamweaver MX)? In the Dreamweaver MX workspace, the Insert bar appears tabbed for each category, whereas the Dreamweaver 4 workspace option displays the Insert bar vertically—you guessed it—as it did in Dreamweaver 4. Mac users get to pick the orientation of the Insert bar without changing workspaces. Look closely at the lower-right corner of the Insert bar and you will see a tiny little button that when clicked toggles the panel from horizontal to vertical and vice versa. If you're so inclined, the vertical Insert bar size can be adjusted by dragging out the corner as you would to change a window's size. Though by doing this you could make it horizontally oriented, you will not get the tabs like in the MX workspace.

TAKING MEASURES

By default, the rulers start at zero in the upper left of the Document window. If you've set your page margins to a value other than zero, you may want the rulers to start where your page starts. You can adjust the rulers by dragging the ruler-origin icon (located where the horizontal and vertical rulers meet in the upper-left corner of the Document window) to the desired coordinates. You'll see a set of crosshairs that indicate the origin position relative to the page. To return the origins to their default values, merely double-click the ruler-origin icon and they'll snap back into place.

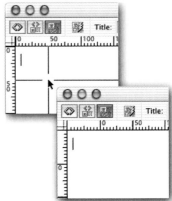

Use the View > Rulers submenu to toggle the rulers on and off, reset the origin (as described previously), or change their unit of measurement to pixels (the default), inches, or centimeters.

CHANGING THE LAYOUT OF THE SITEMAP TO VERTICAL

By default, the Site Map in Dreamweaver displays its icons horizontally; with a site of any size, you're constantly scrolling left and right to find the right branch. I prefer a vertical orientation for my site maps—I find they're especially helpful when I'm saving the map as a graphic. Here's how you switch from a horizontal to a vertical site map:

(1) Expand the Site panel and get into Site Map view.

(2) Double-click the name of your site in the Site drop-down list.

(3) Select the Site Map Layout category on the left. (If you don't see categories on the left, click the Advanced tab at the top.)

(4) Here's the main move: Change the number of columns to 1 from the default of 200, restricting the site map to a single, vertical column.

(5) Increase the Column Width from 125 to about 300. Changing this value lessens the chance that your filenames will bump into the connecting lines. You may have to play with this number to get it just right.

(6) Click OK to close the Site Definition dialog and, voilà—view the vertical site map.

FATAL EXCEPTION: LAST BREATH

If ever you encounter a "Fatal Exception" error in Dreamweaver, don't panic. All is usually not lost—just be sure that you do not click OK or press Enter (Return); otherwise, Dreamweaver will close without letting you save any unsaved documents. When the error appears, ignore it, and click inside the document. The error message will be minimized. It is not a good idea to attempt to continue working; instead, select File > Save for each document that you want to save before Dreamweaver takes its last breath and shuts itself down. After you've saved all of your work, go ahead and maximize the error dialog and click OK. A message dialog with only an OK button may appear. After you click OK, Dreamweaver will completely close down. It is a good idea to reboot your computer before launching Dreamweaver again. (Note: Make sure to check Macromedia's website to be sure you're running the latest version of Dreamweaver MX.)

   SHARING YOUR ASSETS

The more sites you develop, the more you'll find elements they have in common. Instead of spending time recreating things like 1×1 pixel transparent GIF images or taking the time to hunt down an asset in one site just to copy it to another site, you can take advantage of a very handy feature in the Assets panel. You have two ways to do this: I prefer the first because it is one less click, which makes it faster and more efficient. Here are the steps:

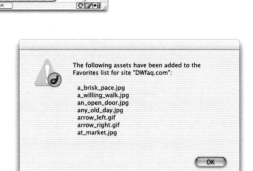

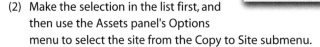

(1) Right-click (Ctrl+click) the asset you want to copy to another site—it doesn't matter which category of the Assets panel you're in—and then select the site listed in the Copy to Site submenu.

(2) Make the selection in the list first, and then use the Assets panel's Options menu to select the site from the Copy to Site submenu.

Oh, but it gets better…You don't have to copy one asset at a time to a site. Within each category of the Assets panel, you can select as many assets as you need to copy. Simply click the first asset and then hold the Shift key while clicking the last asset in a contiguous list, or hold the Ctrl (Command) key while clicking individual assets in the list (Mac: use the Command key). Then use the context menu or the Options menu as described previously to select a site to copy the assets.

After Dreamweaver finishes copying, you'll be alerted with the results of the action; usually, that the assets have been successfully copied to the site and can be found in the Favorites section of the Assets panel for that site.

CODE SPY

I really could have thrown this tip into Chapter 9, "*Pedal to the Metal:* Cool Coding Tips," because it is related to hand coding to some extent. I didn't do that because I really feel it is great advice that I don't want anyone to miss—not that you won't be reading this entire book. But the sooner you start doing this, the better off you'll be.

I want you to spy on your code. That's right—spy on it. Dreamweaver lets you choose between Code view, Design view, or Code and Design view by clicking the respective buttons in the Document toolbar or by selecting the view of choice from one of the first three entries in the View menu. Unless you have good reason, your code should always be visible to you while you're working. Why? Because I said so. Is that not a good enough answer? Oh, okay—I'll tell you why…there's much more to good web development than what you see in Design view. Learning what powers your page, the code, will help you to become a much better developer. When it comes time to troubleshoot a problem, you'll know where to look. Even if you don't know any code at all to start, by watching Dreamweaver create the code for you, eventually the code will start making sense as you become more familiar with it. Before long, you'll be getting your toes wet, so to speak, and eventually you'll dive into the code to do your own customizations.

DESIGN ON TOP

Dreamweaver's workspace is quite flexible. Many workspace layouts are possible so that you can work comfortably and, ultimately, effectively.

Not only do you have the option to work in Code and Design views simultaneously, but you also can choose to have Design view on top when working with both views. You must be in Code and Design view already in order to select View > Design View on Top.

  PLOTTING THE GRID

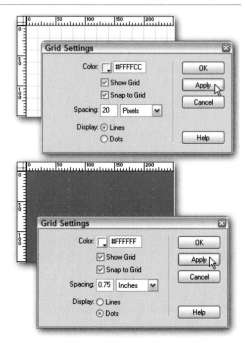

When you are designing with absolute positioned `<div>` tags—known as Layers in Dreamweaver, you will find that the grid can come in very handy. Choose View > Grid > Show Grid or press Ctrl+Alt+G (Command+Option+G) to toggle the grid on and off. The default grid is set to 50-pixel increments in a tan color. This default setting may not be useful for your particular design; especially if you'll be taking advantage of the Snap to Grid feature (also enabled via the View > Grid submenu).

By now, you should have noticed there is a third entry in the View > Grid submenu: Grid Settings. Grid Settings lets you alternately enable and disable the grid itself or the snapping feature; create your grid in the color you want; use pixels, centimeters, or inches; and display the grid as lines or dots. I have found that when the increment is smaller than the default—for example, 20 pixels or less—lines tend to be a better choice because they are easier on the eyes than a bunch of tiny little dots. When I need a larger grid, I like to use dots so that I'm not distracted by the solid lines. If you're using inches, you can even enter decimal values, such as .75 for a 3/4-inch measurement. Don't forget to click the Apply button to see your choices in action, and after you're satisfied, click OK.

LOCAL LEFTY, REMOTE RIGHTY

The (expanded) Site panel lists your local site files on the right and remote files on the left. Many FTP clients are set up just the opposite, with your local files on the left and remote on the right. If you're used to that setup, you could get confused and potentially overwrite files, resulting in loss of work. Don't let this happen to you! If you're accustomed to remote files being on the right side, set Dreamweaver up the same way.

To change the Site panel to display local files on the left, select Edit > Preferences (Dreamweaver > Preferences on Mac OS X) or press Ctrl+U (Command+U) and then click Site in the list of categories on the left side of the Preferences dialog. Now you should see at the top of the dialog the option that allows you to view local files on the right or left. Changing it to read, "Always Show Remote Files on the Left" is the same as leaving it set to, "Always Show Local Files on the Right," so you should change only one list value and not the other. Otherwise, the Site panel will remain the same. Click OK to close the dialog.

   THE USUAL SUSPECTS

This isn't so much a tip as it is a little secret. Ever wonder who's behind the creation of this awesome Dreamweaver program? Get out your magnifying glass because their pictures are small and hidden in the Property inspector. Click any image in a document while in Design view. Open the Property inspector if it is not already visible by

pressing Ctrl+F3 (Command+F3). Ctrl+double-click (Command+double-click) repeatedly on the image thumbnail in the upper left of the Property inspector to cycle through the pictures of Macromedia engineers and other odd images. Foghorn the chicken is kinda cute, don't you think? We may never know the real identity of "hateful-missy," such a shame…

HIDDEN GAME

Hidden deep within the
Dreamweaver interface is a fun
little game you can play when
your boss isn't looking. Careful
though—it is rather addictive.
Select Commands > Create Web
Photo Album and when the
dialog appears, type **play a
game** in the Photo Album Title
field. Press Enter (Return) or
click OK and the Game dialog
appears. If you're familiar with
this color guessing game, have at
it; otherwise, click the Help button to view directions.
I've solved the game in only two guesses at my best,
but I wasn't really trying…so good luck!

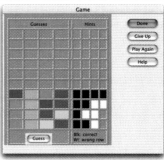

   ### MAXIMUM PANEL HEIGHT

Double-clicking the Panel group title bar is just a little quicker
than using the Options menu to choose Maximize Panel Group. This
will minimize all other expanded Panel groups (if any) within the
docking area and expand the current Panel group to the maximum
available height.

BYPASS OBJECT DIALOG BOXES

Even though you can disable object dialogs by removing the check from the Show Dialog when Inserting Objects checkbox in the General category of Preferences, I prefer to allow the dialogs to always be shown, and then bypass dialogs on a case-by-case basis. (Accessibility dialogs, if enabled in your Accessibility preferences, will always 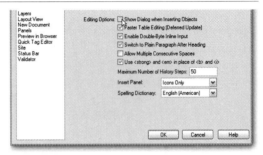 show despite bypassing the main object dialog. If a dialog is not shown, the default values for the object are inserted into the code for that object.) When you Ctrl+click (Command+click) an object, the dialog will be bypassed just as though you had disabled the preference option. (If you did disable the dialogs, the same shortcuts previously noted will enable a dialog.) One case where this comes in especially useful is when you are using the Insert Table object. Dreamweaver stores the information each time you fill out the dialog, so that the next time you see the dialog it is populated with the previously entered values.

For instance, after you've used the Insert Table dialog, the next time you Ctrl+click (Command+click) the Insert Table object, the Insert Table dialog box will not appear. Instead, the values you previously entered in the Insert Table dialog will be inserted automatically into the page. You can bypass the dialog of many objects in this way (but not all of them), so feel free to explore each object to see the result of your bypass attempts.

TILING WINDOWS

After you've picked out your favorite ceramic tile, mix some mortar and then spread it along the base of the window. Then you can begin tiling your window. Wait—this isn't *Martha Stewart* magazine!

Sorry, Mac users, this tip doesn't work for you or the Dreamweaver 4 workspace either. Looking at two or more documents at the same time for comparison purposes is a common occurrence for me. With Dreamweaver MX's new Multiple Document Interface (MDI) for maximized documents, most of the time I can just click the different filename tabs to see what I need to see. Sometimes, however, I really need to see all documents onscreen at the same time. This is when Tiling Windows is especially useful.

Choose Window > Tile Horizontally to set up documents side by side or Window > Tile Vertically so that the documents are set up one above the other. Here's what you need to know: You can tile up to three documents horizontally or vertically, depending on your choice. Four documents will be laid out the same, no matter what your choice and any more than that, well I'll just let you figure it out. If you've minimized a document, it won't be included in the tiling. After you've tiled the documents to your liking, you can easily compare them or copy/paste between them.

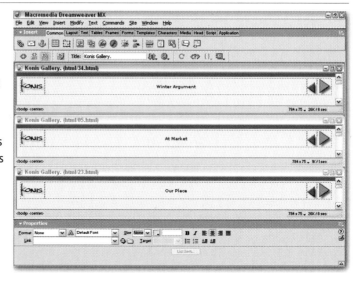

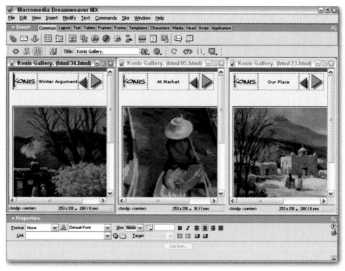

CASCADING STYLE WINDOWS

No, this tip has
nothing to do
with Cascading
Style Sheets—
that's the next
chapter. This tip is
about window
layout in your
Dreamweaver MX
workspace. Sorry,
Mac users; here's
another tip that
doesn't work
for you or the
Dreamweaver 4
workspace.

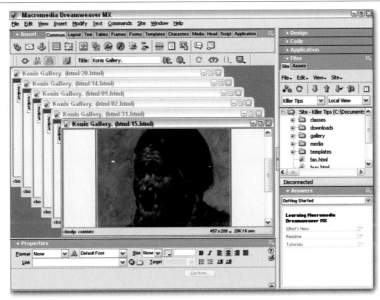

Cascading win-
dows are multiple Dreamweaver Document windows that are overlaid on one another and
offset by about 25 pixels top and left. This layout gives you a small exposed area in the
lower-left and upper-right corner of the document that you can click when you need to
switch between documents. The document you click snaps to the front. By choosing this
method, you're not spending time minimizing and maximizing each document while you
work. All you need to do is select Window > Cascade and your documents will be neatly
tiled with an offset—equally sized, even!

SAME SHORTCUTS GET ANY PANEL YOU WANT!

Sorry Mac users, this tip is for Windows only. Each panel has its very own keyboard shortcut—all of which are listed beside their entry in the Window menu. Most of us won't ever bother to learn every shortcut, even though that would increase our workflow. That's okay; you really don't need to know every single panel shortcut. As long as you know a few easy shortcuts, you can get to any panel you need.

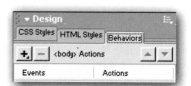

Ctrl+Alt+Tab will display the first Panel group, indicated by dashed lines around the Panel group title. Each time you press the shortcut, you'll move focus to the next Panel group. Use Ctrl+Alt+Shift+Tab to move backward through the Panel groups. You can use the arrow keys to maneuver between Panel groups, but pressing the arrow keys will only move the focus between Panel groups in the same column. To expand a Panel group press the space-bar. If a Panel group is already expanded, you can reach the Options menu by first pressing the right-arrow key and then the spacebar. Use your up- and down-arrow keys to move through the list and then press Enter to make a selection.

Now that the Panel group is open, you can use the arrow keys or Tab between panels. Use the right- or left-arrow keys to go to the next panel in the group. Now that you're at the panel you want, you should see focus lines around the name of the panel on its tab. Press the Tab key to move between options in the Panel group. Generally, you'll use the spacebar to press buttons, the up- and down-arrow keys to move through lists, and Enter to make a selection. If your mouse breaks, you're prepared!

CLEAN YOUR WORKSPACE

I'm not asking you to clean your desktop, virtual or otherwise—just your Dreamweaver environment. There are certain panels you may never need or find yourself using rarely enough that you needn't keep them in their Panel group. In a few simple steps, you can get that panel out of its group and out of your sight for good—or at least until you need it again.

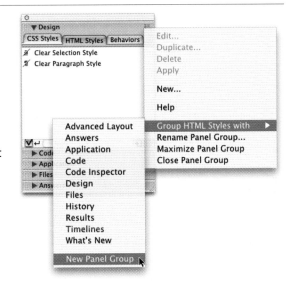

In the next chapter, you'll learn so many cool things about CSS that you'll feel the same way about the HTML Styles panel as I do. Don't wait until then to do this, however; you may as well ditch that HTML Styles panel now. Here's how you do it:

(1) Make the HTML Styles panel visible if it isn't already—you'd better be selecting Window > HTML Styles, because if you memorized the keyboard shortcut, you may as well just forget it!

(2) Open the Options menu and select Group HTML Styles with > New Panel Group. The panel will detach itself from the current Panel group and the title of the panel (in this case, HTML Styles) will become the Panel group's title.

(3) Close the Panel group by choosing Close Panel Group from the Options menu or by closing it as you would any normal window.

If you're never going to be using ColdFusion, you'll never need the Components panel. You can close any other panel you feel you don't need or re-open and re-dock the ones you've closed. I prefer a cleaner workspace with only the tools I use regularly in sight at any given time. Doesn't that feel better now? Good—now you can go clean your office!

   FASTER SITE OPERATIONS

If you're like me, you prefer to keep your source files (such as Fireworks PNG files and Flash FLA files) in your site definition so that you always know where to find them. Uploading these files is usually not a good idea because it exposes them to other people, who may be inclined to use them. Accidentally uploading these files can be avoided with Dreamweaver MX's new cloaking feature.

Cloaking isn't just for source files but any folder or file extension that you want to exclude from site operations, which in turn will speed up site operations. For example, cloaked image files will not appear in the Assets panel, which improves its load time. Right-click (Ctrl+click) the folder you want to cloak and select Cloaking > Cloak (unless it is dimmed, in which case you must choose Enable Cloaking instead and then come back and choose Cloak). A red slash indicates that a folder and all files contained in it are now cloaked.

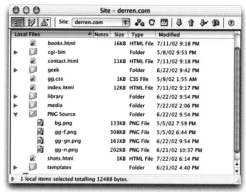

From that same context menu, you can choose Settings, which will open your site definition right to the Cloaking category where you can enable the feature to cloak files with the specified file extension. You can add file extensions to the list separated by a space to tell Dreamweaver which types of files you want to cloak; just be sure to include the dot prior to the extension. All cloaked files will be indicated by a red slash through its icon. Be careful if you choose Uncloak All from the context menu because after you do that, if you need the files cloaked again you'll have to do it manually. It is usually a better choice to just temporarily disable cloaking.

DREAMWEAVER 4 AND THE MACINTOSH SITE PANEL

The Dreamweaver 4 workspace option and the Mac do not dock the Site panel as a tabbed panel. But that doesn't mean you can't take advantage of the Site panel in the same ways you can in the MX workspace; it just means you need some creative setup of your workspace and a little bit of practice.

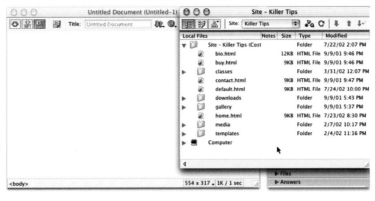

If it isn't already visible, open the Site panel by pressing F8. Now look way down in the bottom-left corner of the Site panel. Do

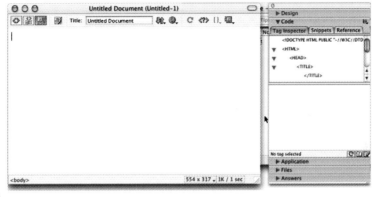

you see that little arrow icon? Go ahead and click it. The Site panel will collapse to the width of the Local Site area of the panel. Click the arrow again and it will expand—no surprise there. What you should remember is that if you're going to reduce the width of the collapsed panel, you should actually reduce the width of the Local Site area by the divider instead. If you change the width after it is collapsed, and then expand and collapse it once more, the adjusted width is not retained. Move your Panel groups away from where you will next be dragging the Site panel (by the title bar) over to the right or left of the Document window. After you have the Site panel in place, move your Panel groups over the Site panel but allow them to hang past the Site panel just a little.

Now that I've got you all set up, look at how simple it is to switch to the Site panel and back to the panels. Because a sliver of the Site panel or Panel groups is always visible to you no matter which is in focus, all you need to do is click that area to bring the panel to the front.

WHO SAYS IT IS RUDE TO POINT?

Your mother may tell you it is rude to point, but Dreamweaver enthusiasts would certainly disagree. The ultimate way to create links within your site using Dreamweaver is known as the "point-to-file" technique. Touch your text or image with your index finger; then touch the file you want to link to in the Site panel. Okay, I'm pulling your leg again—not your finger—but the process is *almost* that simple.

Make your selection in Design or Code view, and then look on the Property inspector or the Tag inspector's property sheet value fields for the point-to-file icon (this is usually found to the left of the Browse for File folder icon, which you will be using less and less after this tip). Click and drag from the icon and you'll see an arrow with a line emerge from the icon that follows your mouse to the file you want to become the hyperlink. The file that you point to can be in the Site panel or another open document. After you release the mouse button, an <a> tag wraps your selection and makes the file you pointed to the href value of the tag. You can make hyperlinks as fast as you can click and drag, but browsing endlessly for a file is much more of a drag, don't you agree?

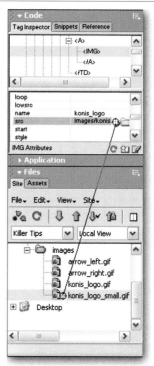

Speed, Grace, and Style

Just think of how much faster your web pages would be if you didn't use any <font> tags… This chapter is packed with all sorts of cool CSS

Speed, Grace, and Style

power css tips

(Cascading Style Sheet) tricks. Some tips work in older browsers and some do not; the cooler the tip, the more likely it is only for modern browsers, such as Internet Explorer 5+ and Netscape 6+. Keep in mind that it is rare that someone—other than web developers or clients—will see your page in both older browsers and modern ones; typically, the general public uses only one browser or another and will never compare the site between browsers. Don't drive yourself crazy making everything identical across browsers or platforms. All that really matters is that the site looks acceptable and is fully functional.

You're on your own to test drive the CSS in the browsers that matter most to you and use them where appropriate. For the most part, we're not going to worry about what is or is not proprietary CSS or "valid" to CSS standards. My goal is to open you up to the possibilities that CSS has to offer. Although a few of these tips may be ahead of their time and not practical for you now, I'm betting they will prove valuable to you in the future.

DESIGN TIME STYLE SHEETS

Design Time Style Sheets has to be in my top 10 favorite new features of Dreamweaver MX. If you've ever opened Server-Side Includes (SSI) or Library Items that use CSS, you'll know that in Design view, you can't see the applied CSS or make use of the CSS Styles panel.

As long as the document has been previously saved, you may choose the CSS Panel's Options menu to select Design Time Style Sheets. You also can right-click (Command+click) in the CSS Styles panel to display the same Design Time Style Sheets option. When the Design Time Style Sheets dialog appears, you can click the Add (+) button to browse to and select the CSS file you need. You can even choose to exclude CSS files that are already linked to the file so that they are not shown in Design view, but because they are still part of the code, will show in the browser. You can search through the document if you like, but you won't see any reference to the CSS file in the code at all. In addition to SSIs and Library Items, Design Time Style Sheets also come in handy when a style sheet is dynamically assigned.

   PATH TO SUCCESS

The way a path is written is important in successfully showing an image declared with CSS in Netscape 4.x. Although using a relative path like `../images/myimage.gif` is perfectly legitimate, Netscape 4.x often gets confused by document relative paths. Save yourself the debugging headaches and make it a habit to always use root relative paths, such as `/assets/images/myimage.gif`. Alternatively, you can use absolute paths. Either root relative or absolute paths will guarantee that your images will be found and displayed.

@import TRICK

A simple way to avoid all the hassles of browser sniffing and redirects to multiple versions of the same site is to use what is known as the `@import` trick. What you need to do is create one style sheet that works well for all browsers

and create another one containing a CSS for modern browsers, which is called upon `@import`. Older browsers, such as Netscape 4.x, do not recognize `@import` and completely ignore it. This means that you can put all the cool CSS properties into that style sheet and essentially hide it from Netscape 4.x. When you attach a style sheet by clicking the Attach Style Sheet icon, you will see a radio button option for Link or Import. The procedure is as simple as choosing the CSS file, selecting the Import option, and clicking OK. Keep in mind that the `@import` style sheet must come after a linked style sheet. The link-first, import-second order is needed to override the CSS rules assigned to the same selectors for older browsers because being second makes that CSS more "import"ant.

   ### CSS SHORTHAND

You can write CSS out the long way, like this:

```
body {
        margin-top: 12px;
        margin-right: 12px;
        margin-bottom: 12px;
        margin-left: 12px;
}
```

Or you can write it out the short-hand way, like this:

```
body {
  margin: 12px;
}
```

You either need to know CSS shorthand so you can hand-code it (Eek!) or you can let Dreamweaver handle it all for you (Whew!). Look under the CSS Styles category of Edit > Preferences (Dreamweaver > Preferences on Mac OS X) or press Ctrl+U (Command+U) and you will find the options for using shorthand. You can use shorthand for all of the checked property types or you can set it to use shorthand only if that is how the code was originally written. All CSS written or modified from now on will use the chosen formatting, but existing CSS remains in original format.

DEFINITION SHARING

When you have multiple elements that have certain styles in common—such as color, size, or font family—you can save a whole lot of code by declaring everything altogether. Let's say you have the following three defined styles:

```
body {
  font-family: Verdana, Arial, Helvetica, sans-serif;
  font-size: 12px;
  color: #CCCCCC;
  background-color: #330066;
  }
p {
  font-family: Verdana, Arial, Helvetica, sans-serif;
  font-size: 12px;
  color: #333333;
}

td {
    font-family: Verdana, Arial, Helvetica, sans-serif;
    font-size: 12px;
}
```

You can combine these styles to share their common definitions, using commas to separate each element as shown here:

```
body, td, p{
  font-family: Verdana, Arial, Helvetica, sans-serif;
  font-size: 12px;
}
body {
  color: #CCCCCC;
  background-color: #330066;
  }
p {
  color: #333333;
  }
```

Click the New CSS Style icon to use Dreamweaver's interface to add these styles. You'll want to do your single elements first using the Redefine HTML option. To add multiple elements through Dreamweaver's interface, select the Use CSS Selector radio button and enter each element separated by a comma in the Selector field at the top of the dialog. If you try to define a single element that has already been used in a multiple element definition, Dreamweaver will make the "No you can't do that" sound and show an error saying that the element has already been defined. You may just find that it is easier to combine styles manually after you've defined all your CSS.

CAN I SEE SOME IDENTIFICATION, PLEASE?

You can give just about any HTML element an ID attribute to use with CSS to style that element. ID values must be unique to the document; you can't use the same ID more than once on a page or you'll run into trouble. CSS offers ID selectors, which automatically apply the CSS to the element containing an ID that matches it. Take a look at this code, for example:

```
#content {
color: #333333;
}
```

In the document you could have something like:

```
<p id="content">Some text here</p>
```

That particular paragraph would be displayed with the color specified by the `#content` definition. In the New CSS Style dialog, you'll need to choose the Use CSS Selector radio button for the field to accept the `#` that indicates ID selectors.

MARGIN MADNESS

You've got your page design all laid out, and there is only one thing keeping it from looking its best: it doesn't sit snug against the left and top edges of the browser window. I like to think of a browser as a printer. This helps me remember that, just like setting up a page to be printed, I have to specify the margins of web pages, too.

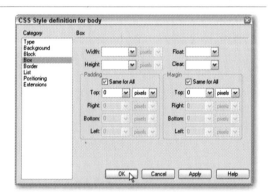

Select the Redefine HTML Tag radio button in the New CSS Style dialog, and then type **body** in the Tag field or select it from the list. In the Box category of the CSS Style Definition dialog, you can set margin and padding to whatever values you choose. For the most part, margin values are what you really need, and the padding property will take care of Opera browsers. If satisfying Netscape 4.x is an absolute must, you also can set the `marginwidth` and `marginheight` attributes in the `<body>` tag by choosing Modify > Page Properties and entering the settings you want in the dialog.

COMPUTER CLONING

Recently I discovered that with a little bit of CSS, I can make a web page closely resemble the screen of the user's very own computer. Start your wheels turning and think of the possibilities this brings you! Many computer users will set their system in such a way that is most comfortable for them, especially people who are visually impaired. Any color or background-color can be assigned a system color value. For example, try this code:

```
body {
background-color: Background;
}
```

Hmm, does that resemble your desktop's color? There are too many possible values to list and describe here, but you can find all of them on the web at www.w3.org/TR/REC-CSS2/ ui.html#system-colors.

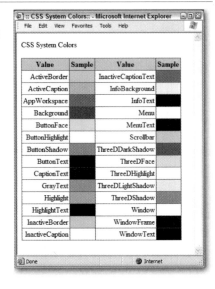

Dreamweaver's CSS Style Definition dialog will tell you that the value you entered is not a valid color, even though it really is so you'll have to hand-code it. Oh, and don't expect to see these values represented in Dreamweaver's Design view, either; they'll work only in the browser. Keep in mind that if you use a system color for a background, it is wise to use a system color for the text color too. If you specify a color, such as black, and their background just so happens to be black, then the user won't see the text at all!

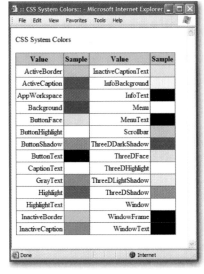

FONT TAGS? FUGGEDABOUDIT…

You just fuggedaboudit. Resist all temptation to use deprecated font tags. You already learned from the tip in Chapter 1 titled "Clean Your Workspace" how to get rid of the HTML Styles panel. Now it is time for you to knock off font tags for good. Hidden in the Property inspector is a new CSS mode that replaces the need for `<font>` and its attributes: face, size, and

color, and the align attribute placed on other elements such as `<p>` or `<td>`. You can either click the A icon to the left of the font-family list or choose CSS Mode from the Options menu.

After you're in CSS mode, you can apply available custom classes, add new styles, edit existing styles, or

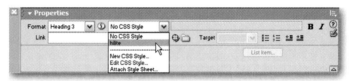

even attach style sheets by using the drop-down list to the right of the CSS icon.

CLASSY BUT CAREFUL

This tip is especially helpful when you're working with a team that is inclined to apply classes all over the place. Some custom classes would wreak havoc on your design if they were not properly applied. This can be especially true for the styling of form buttons. Here's an example of CSS that is applied only to an

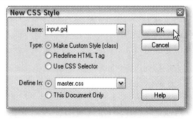

`<input>` tag with the class attribute equal to `go`. Notice that the format is element dot custom class and must be entered in the New CSS Style dialog with the Use CSS Selector radio button chosen.

```
input.go {
font:bold 13px Verdana,Arial,Helvetica,sans-serif;
color:#333333;
background:#CDD5DC;
border:1px #06334B outset;
}
```

As long as the .go class is not defined elsewhere in your style sheet, it doesn't matter whether the designer adds `class="go"` to every element on the page. The only element that would be affected by it is the `<input>` tag. That'll teach those designers not to be class-happy! Oh, and just for the record, this is one style definition that you'll want to hide from Netscape 4.x browsers because of the border.

 **CSS ANCESTORY**

Let's say that you want only paragraphs that are inside a table cell to be affected by your style rule. You start with the parent element and work down the family tree to the element you need by using what is known as a *contextual selector*. In our case, the code would look something like:

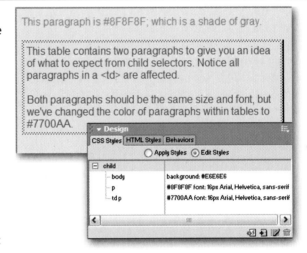

```
td p {
color: #333300;
}
```

You could get even more specific and change only the color of a paragraph's text if the `<td>` has a specific class already applied. (See the tip, earlier in this chapter, "Classy but Careful"). Because spaces are not allowed in the other two options, you'll once be again choosing the Use CSS Selector radio button.

 INSTANT CSS FILE

Who says you must already have a CSS file to link it to the document? Certainly not me! Whichever way you choose to attach a style sheet, be it via the Attach Style Sheet icon, the Attach Style Sheet command in the CSS Styles panel's Options menu or a context menu, or

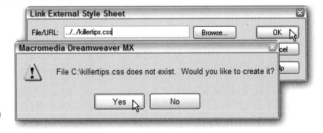

even from the drop-down list in the CSS mode of the Property inspector, you'll be prompted by the Link External Style Sheet dialog. Don't worry if you don't already have a CSS file; just type the path to the file as though it already exists and click OK. Dreamweaver will tell you that the file doesn't exist and ask whether you'd like to create it. Naturally, your answer is Yes. This saves you the time of creating a style sheet first and then coming back to link it. I love these little timesavers, don't you?

ROUNDING THE CORNERS

Shave off those sharp table edges with a little bit of CSS. That's right—CSS can even round off table corners. The code is proprietary for Mozilla and Netscape 6.x and higher, but it leaves Internet Explorer with normal sharp tables. You'll be able to use Dreamweaver's CSS editor for all but the snippet of code that does the rounding. Create a new style using the Redefine HTML Tag option, and select `table` from the list of tags. Proceed as usual to the CSS Style Definition dialog. There you can choose a background color,

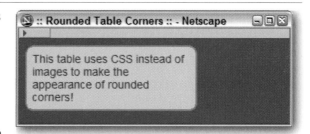

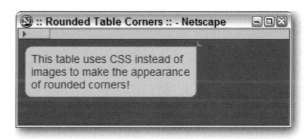

a border size, and a color for the table. When you're satisfied, click OK. Here's the line of code you'll need to enter manually at the end of the table style rule you just defined:

```
-moz-border-radius: 12px;
```

Don't forget to add that starting dash, or the code won't work! Why does it have to be the last declaration in the style rule? If you don't add it last, other declarations in the rule may not show up in Design view or the preview area of the Edit Styles mode in the CSS Styles panel. In Design view, you won't see anything unusual. It's not until you look at the page in a supporting browser that you'll see the rounded corners. The edges can sometimes look jagged, but I find that some colors work better together than others do. I hope that there will be better support for this cool CSS in future browsers.

For extra fun, try this little twist on the same concept, which makes use of a negative value:

```
-moz-border-radius-topright: -12px;
-moz-border-radius-topleft: 10px;
-moz-border-radius-bottomright: 10px;
-moz-border-radius-bottomleft: 10px;
```

   JUST SNIPPET

There are many properties that the CSS Style Definition dialog doesn't address at all. One of the more popular pieces of CSS code is the one used to make colored scrollbars in Internet Explorer 5.5+ on Windows. Code like that is perfect for storing in the Snippets panel so that you've got it when you need it, and you may not need to waste time hunting down the code. I'll even give you the code so you have something to play with:

```
html{ /*Define the <html> tag (not <body>) so that it you're using a
DOCTYPE with URI, the colors still show*/
scrollbar-highlight-color:#C2C2DA;
scrollbar-shadow-color:#8D8DC7;
scrollbar-track-color:#272752;
scrollbar-face-color:#474792;
scrollbar-arrow-color:#E8E8F4;
scrollbar-darkshadow-color:#000000;
scrollbar-3dlight-color:#272752;
}
```

Keep in mind that if the CSS Style Definition dialog doesn't have the CSS you need, Dreamweaver won't display it, and it is probably proprietary code that has limited browser support. Look close at the comment tag in the code above for a hidden little tip.

   INVISIBLE INK

You can control the visibility of nearly any element with a little bit of CSS. You've probably seen the code if you've ever drawn a layer in Design view and then changed its visibility in the Property inspector or Layers panel. There are three possible values to the `visibility` property: `visible`, `hidden`, and `inherit`. I think you can figure what the first two do; the third value, `inherit`, is not so obvious. `inherit` simply means that it will take (or inherit) the same value as its parent element. With some JavaScript knowledge, you can turn an element's visibility on and off. You'll find the `visibility` property in the Positioning category of the CSS Style Definition dialog.

FILTERED OR NON-FILTERED?

You can create the illusion of some cool effects without altering an image in an editor such as Fireworks. Mind you, this isn't for everyone—it is Internet Explorer proprietary. But if that doesn't matter, you can have a load of fun. Check out the Filter drop-down list in the Extensions category of the CSS Style Definition dialog. You'll find an effect that turns a color image to black and white, an effect that makes an image look like

an x-ray, and a whole lot more. You can use the filters on plain normal images, or for extra fun, combine them with JavaScript. Here's an example of a CSS that uses the `Invert` effect when you place your pointer over an image that is a hyperlink:

```
.scary a:hover img {
filter: Invert;
}
```

Here's what the code might look like in the document:

```
<div id="Festival" class="scary"><a href="festival.htm"><img
src="festival.jpg" width="450" height="229" border="0"></a></div>
```

`Invert` gives it a sort of creepy look, somewhat like a film negative. Remember that because these filters are proprietary, they won't validate as CSS. Since we are using a contextual selector, it must be entered in the New CSS Style dialog with the Use CSS Selector radio button chosen. Don't forget to apply the class to your HTML element, in our case that's a `<div>`.

HANDY POINTER

Browser support for the cursor property varies significantly between Internet Explorer and Netscape 6+. What Windows Internet Explorer 5.x knows as the *hand*, Netscape 6+, Internet Explorer 6, and Macintosh Internet Explorer 5 calls the *pointer*. So how do we make both browsers happy and still get the cursor we desire? It's simple, actually. Whenever there is a conflict, the closest style definition wins. This tip gives you a prime example of how you can use this to your advantage. Let's create a custom class called `.mouse`. On the left of the CSS Style Definition dialog, click Extensions. Now select `hand` from the Cursor drop-down list. Now in Code view, you'll need to add `pointer` because Netscape doesn't recognize `hand`, like so:

```
.mouse {
cursor: pointer;
cursor: hand;
}
```

If you flip that order, Internet Explorer will be looking for `pointer`, which it doesn't understand. You won't get the desired results. There isn't anything illegal about using the same property twice in a rule; however, because the `hand` value is not valid CSS, the style sheet won't validate. So use this handy pointer when you feel it is appropriate.

COUNTERFEIT WEB PAGES

Watermarks used to help prove authenticity or serve as branding on currency and official documents are quite common nowadays. Somehow, someone got the idea that a similar look could be given to websites. Although it isn't entirely cross-browser, `background-attachment:fixed;` when used with the `<body>` or `<div>` tag works well for this purpose. (You'll find it in the Background category of the CSS Style Definition dialog with all the other background properties.) When you scroll the page in modern browsers, a declared background-image will remain onscreen. In Netscape 4.x, the background is thrown into the upper-left corner and will move—not remain onscreen—when the page is scrolled. By now, you know that you can avoid showing a style in Netscape 4.x by using the "`@import` Trick" tip given earlier in this chapter.

COLLAPSING BORDERS

Applying borders to a table and all its cells using CSS isn't as simple as it may seem. Go ahead and try it. Create a 3 × 3 table and try to create the CSS you need to outline each cell with a single pixel line. You can find border options in the Border category of the CSS Style Definition dialog. Your first attempt may look something like this if you've set all borders equally and are using shorthand:

```
table, td, th {
border: 1px solid #000000;
}
```

When you view this in Dreamweaver or the browser, you will see that borders appear to be two pixels thick. Keep trying if you'd like but unless you know this code, you're going to end up with a whole lot more CSS than you really need to do the job. The `border-collapse: collapse;`—it isn't an option in the CSS Style Definition dialog—declaration added to the preceding code or applied to a `<table>` via custom class will do the job.

Dreamweaver's Design view doesn't support the border-collapse property, and if the `<table>` tag doesn't have cell spacing set to 0, the lack of support in Design view is even more obvious. Modern browsers, such as Internet 5.x+, Netscape 6.x+ and Opera 5.x+, all support the property. You will run into some problems, however, if you have empty cells in your table. Other minor caveats apply as well. Remember to test in the browsers that matter most to you.

  ### IT'S A LOVE/HATE RELATIONSHIP

I do whatever it takes to remember coding techniques. I'm not sure who originally thought of this one, but it is simple to remember: LoVe HAte. The capital letters represent the first letter in each of the pseudoclasses used to control hyperlink styles. For the cascade to work the way most users would expect it to, the order of these pseudoclasses is very important:

`a:link`, `a:visited`, `a:hover`, `a:active`. You'll find each one listed in the proper order in the Selector drop-down list when you've chosen Use CSS Selector in the New CSS Style dialog. In the correct order, one by one, you'll define their rules. When you're finished, you should have code similar to the following:

```
a:link {
color: #3C679B;
}
a:visited{
color: #7193BD;
}
a:hover {
color: #274365;
}
a:active{
color: #9771BD;
}
```

   ### SIMPLIFYING THE SWITCHEROO

One of the questions I am asked most often regarding CSS is why I have used multiple style sheets for each page at `DWfaq.com`. DWfaq.com offers the user the capability to set their preferred style in the My DWfaq menu. When you are designing a site that will be switching styles, you'll want to keep as much of the common code as possible in a separate style sheet. This way, when it comes time to change the size of that `<h1>`, you will make the change in the common CSS file rather than changing the `<h1>` in each theme's style sheet. You can link as many style sheets or call as many style sheets using `@import` as you'd like. Keep in mind that if there are conflicting styles between files, whichever style is physically nearest the element wins the dispute. Another bonus to this method is that if the browser caches the common style sheet, only the new theme's style needs to be downloaded, which can help speed up your page's load time.

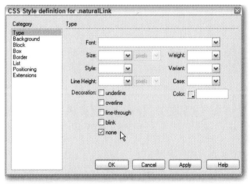

INHERITING THE FAMILY FORTUNE

When it comes to CSS, understanding inheritance will really help you soar as a developer. Essentially the *cascade* in Cascading Style Sheets is all about inheritance. In theory, when you are applying a font-family to an element, its children will inherit that font-family. The `<body>` tag, being the parent element of all other tags, should pass along its declared font-family to its children. Unfortunately, Netscape 4.x doesn't quite get inheritance right, especially when it comes to tables. If you want to make sure that all children get their inheritance, you'd better state it clearly in your last will and testament. When it comes to CSS, because all text in a table will be in either a `<td>` or a `<th>`, you'll want to be sure to explicitly declare values for these elements. Add as many elements as needed to appease Netscape 4.x. Using what you learned in the "Definition Sharing" tip earlier in this chapter, your rule may look something like this:

```
body, td, th {
font-family: Verdana, Arial, Helvetica, sans-serif;
}
```

CAREFULLY REMOVING UNDIES

Removing underlines from links is super simple with CSS. One thing to bear in mind is that visitors rely on underlines to spot links. Unless the non-underlined text is placed in an obvious location, such as a navigation bar, your visitor may not notice them. That said, I can now tell you how to remove underlines. When defining link styles—as described in the "It's a LoVe HAte Relationship" tip earlier in this chapter—add `text-decoration:none` to the rule. You'll find the text-decoration property and its values represented by the group of Decoration checkboxes in the Type category of the CSS Style Definition dialog.

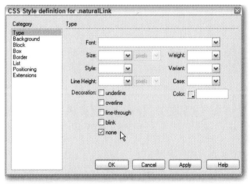

CLICKABLE CELLS THAT CHANGE COLORS

This is another good one to keep handy in your Snippets panel, especially if you make it a habit to name classes the same way for all the sites you develop. Have you ever wondered how to make a clickable cell that changes color when the user places the pointer over that cell? As you may have already guessed, this only works in modern browsers. Here's what you do:

(1) Create a custom class for the rollover effect. I've named mine `.rollover`.

(2) Create a custom class for when the pointer isn't over the cell. I've named this custom class `.plain`.

(3) Apply the `.plain` class to the `<td>` and then hand-code the `onMouseOver` and `onMouseOut` events, as shown in the code here

```
<td class="plain"
onMouseOver=" this.className='rollover';"
onMouseOut=" this.className='plain';">
```

(4) To make the cell clickable, select the `<td>` tag in the Tag Selector and then apply the Go to URL behavior in the Behaviors panel. Be sure the event is set as `onClick`.

(5) For a final touch, add CSS to ensure that the hand/pointer cursor is shown when the user moves the cursor over the cell (as described in the "Handy Pointer" tip earlier in this chapter).

HANDY DANDY TAG SELECTOR

That handy dandy Tag Selector in the lower left of the Document window even helps with custom classes. You may have noticed that if a tag already has a custom class applied, the tag is shown with the custom class using dot notation, like this: `<element.class>`. Similarly, if the tag has an ID , it is represented in the Tag Selector, like this: `<element#id>`.

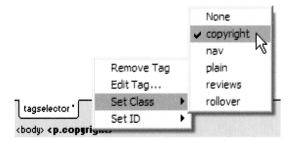

If you right-click (Ctrl+click) a tag in the Tag Selector while in Design view, you will see the Set Class option. In the Set Class submenu, you can apply a style if one hasn't been applied, switch to a new style if a custom class has been applied (indicated by a checkmark), or choose None at the top of the list to remove the style already applied. I happen to prefer this method because it allows me to leave the CSS Styles panel in Edit Styles mode, and I don't need to switch back and forth to the Apply Styles mode because the CSS Styles panel isn't always readily available. Anyhow, the fewer the number of clicks, the faster the job is done, and that's what matters.

   OUT WITH THE OLD STYLES, IN WITH THE NEW

It is time for spring-cleaning and getting rid of unnecessary custom classes applied throughout your document. Maybe you've inherited a document from a previous designer who was class-happy and applied classes willy-nilly throughout the document. Maybe you've just plain changed your mind about how the style should be applied. Whatever your motive, the solution is the same. Select the element(s) in question and then click No CSS Style in the Apply Styles mode of the CSS Styles panel. Any classes that were applied within your selection should now be removed from the code.

A SHORT COMMENTARY

If you have not been using the pre-made CSS files in the New Document dialog under the CSS Style Sheets category, and instead have chosen to create a blank CSS file from the New Document dialog (choose File > New) under the Basic Page category, you'll find that the file starts with a line like this: /* CSS Document */. (*Pssst*, I snuck a tip in there; did you spot that?) If you haven't guessed by now, /* . . .* / denotes a CSS comment. Dreamweaver does not

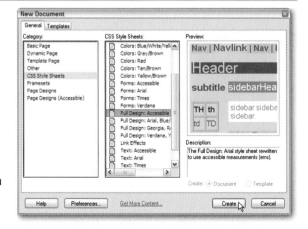

supply an interface for adding comments to CSS files. You can, however, create a snippet designed to wrap your current selection that uses /* for the Insert Before and / for the Insert After fields. I like to add comments to my CSS file to help me remember how and why I used the style definitions. I even use CSS comments to remind myself of browser compatibility issues. Something like this:

```
/*Application: <td> or <p> only
Browsers: IE 5+, NS 6+, Opera 5+ only. Netscape 4.x will not display the
border properly.
Notes: Be sure transparent images look okay against this dark background
color!*/
```

True, this file may get lengthy if it is filled with comments, but you can upload a copy without comments and keep the commented file only for local use.

GO AHEAD, USE ANOTHER EDITOR

If you must use another editor, such as TopStyle,
HomeSite, BBedit or even NotePad, for your CSS—
Dreamweaver won't get its feelings hurt. Select
Edit > Preferences (Dreamweaver > Preferences
on Mac OS X) or Ctrl+U (Command+U) and
then choose File Types/Editors from the list of
categories on the left. Now locate or add the .css
file type in the Extensions list and make sure that
the editor you want to use is listed in the Editors
list. If it's not, use the Add (+) button and browse
to the editor of your choice. To be able to double-
click the CSS file to open it in the external editor,
remove .css from the list of files that open in
Code view. I prefer to leave .css in the list and use
either the right-click (Ctrl+click) context menu or
the Options menu of the CSS Styles panel and
verify that Use External Editor is checked. If it is
checked, when you double-click a style in the CSS
Styles panel, it will open the file in the external
editor specified by your Preferences.

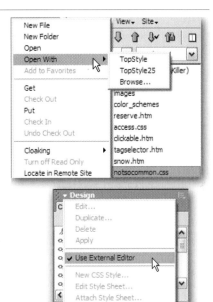

Racin' Down the Rows

Header
Row
Ahead

Remember the first time you looked at the code for a complex table and tried to figure out why it was blowing up on one browser or another? Unless you're

Racin' Down the Rows
the best table tips

weirder than I am—and that's very weird—this is not like reminiscing about your first kiss. It's more like reliving the first fight you had where the school bully spun you over his head like a sack of lemons. (Don't tell me you've missed out on such a quintessential moment of growing up? If you think you have, it's only because you're in complete denial and require several years of regression therapy to recover the memory.) Even if you're moving away from tables as a layout tool, they remain an essential element of most every website for structured data and sliced graphics—and one that you need to master.

The tips in this chapter are designed to put you in the driver's seat when dealing with tables. The full gamut of table-related functionality is fair game here: structured data, formatted tables, layout tables, sliced graphics and more. You'll even find cool ways to work with data from Excel spreadsheets and Word tables. By the time you're finished with this chapter, you should have those tables spinning over your head like the proverbial fruit of your own choosing.

   SELECTING TABLE ROWS AND COLUMNS FOR FUN AND PROFIT

You can substantially reduce the amount of time required for complex tables by mastering table row and column selection. There are a couple of ways you can select a row or column. The fastest one I've found is to click a cell at one end of a row or column and then drag across to the other end. If you're more of a clicker than a dragger, put your cursor in one cell and Shift+click in the last cell—that selects those cells and all the ones in-between. On the Mac, you'll need to Shift+double-click to get the same effect.

Another technique is one of the most flexible, although it is a touch harder to master. Position your cursor on the outer border of a row or column until the single-headed arrow appears; the sweet spot is about 2-pixels wide and only along the left and top borders. Click once and the indicated row or column is selected. To select contiguous rows or columns, get in that one-headed arrow sweet spot and drag across your selection; once you've started dragging, you can move outside the 2-pixel zone. Pretty cool, eh? Even cooler: if you combine the single-click method with the Ctrl (Command) key, you can even select rows that aren't next to each other. This selection method gives you a really fast way to add a background color to alternating rows, for example, without going the Commands > Format Table route.

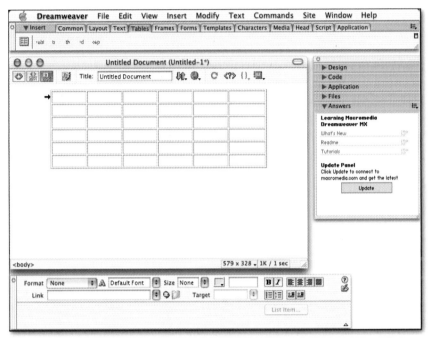

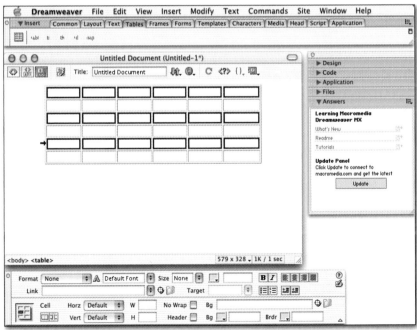

  KEYBOARD SHORTCUTS

Want to play quick draw? You select a table with a mouse and I'll do the same with the keyboard. Ready? Go! Beat ya. How'd I do it? The same keyboard shortcut that is ordinarily used for selecting everything on the page (Ctrl+A, or Command+A on the Mac) works differently within a table. The first time you press the key combination, the current table cell is selected; the second time, the entire table is highlighted. How fast can you hit the same keyboard combination twice in a row? Pretty fast, right?

Want to go again? Okay, this time let's add a row. Ready? Gee…I'm done. That's just how quickly I can press Ctrl+M (Command+M), which inserts a new row above the cursor. Best two out three? How about deleting a row? Whoa—you almost got me that time, but only because I had to do a Ctrl+Shift+M (Command+Shift+M). You can use the equivalent keyboard shortcuts for adding a column (Ctrl+Shift+A, or Command+ Shift+A on the Mac) and deleting one (Ctrl+Shift+Minus, or Command+Shift+Minus).

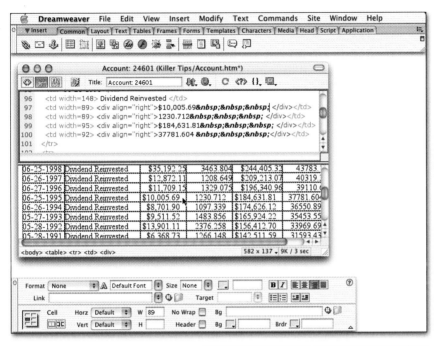

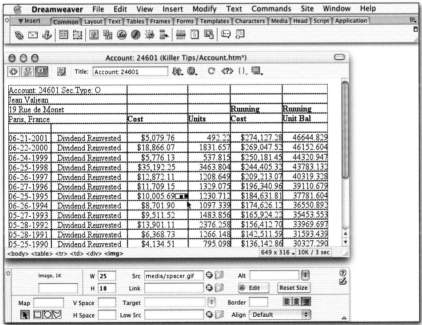

COMPLEX FORMATTING FROM EXCEL

Got a spreadsheet table with a complex bit of formatting you want to webbify? There's no direct route from Excel (or any other spreadsheet, for that matter) to Dreamweaver, but follow me and I can guide you through those rocky shoals. Start out by copying the range of cells in Excel and pasting it into a blank document in Word. Then save the Word doc as a web page—that'll put it in a format that can be brought into Dreamweaver. In

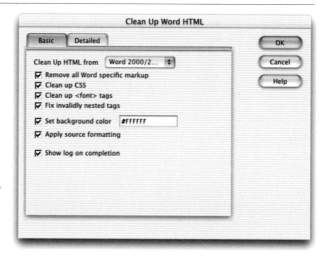

Dreamweaver, choose File > Import > Word HTML and bring in the document. Dreamweaver will automatically pop up the Clean Up Word HTML dialog. Select all the desired options (to tell you the truth, I use them all) and let 'er rip. Now you've got a pretty clean version of a densely formatted table that you can copy and paste wherever you need it. If you just need the data without the fancy-schmancy formatting, use Dreamweaver's Import Tabular Data command.

   SPLITTING HAIRY ROWS

Nobody gets a table layout right the first time. Nobody. Seems like you always have to add a column or merge a row to get just the right setup. Let's say you've got a table with a single cell in the top row and six columns in the rest of the rows—and now you've got to

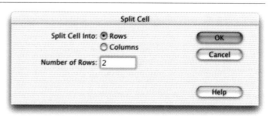

split the top row into two equal cells. When you choose Split Cell from the Property inspector, Dreamweaver displays the dialog and suggests a number of columns to use; typically the maximum number of columns in the table. You might think, "Whoa, that's *way* more than I need; let me dial this puppy back a notch or two." But don't touch that dial! It's far better to split the cell initially into the maximum number of columns and then merge any cells necessary to get the look you need. If you don't do it this way, you'll spend countless hours—okay, well, maybe an extra 10 minutes or so—trying to get it right.

   CUSTOM FORMATS

Have you discovered Commands > Format Table yet? I think it's one of Dreamweaver's niftiest gems. Apply this command to any table chock full of data and faster than you can say, "Bob's your uncle!" (or any obscure English phrase you like), you've got a fully formatted table complete with a nicely styled header row and alternating colored rows.

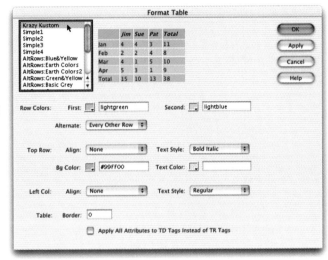

Even though Format Table offers a lot of options—you can customize any of the 17 presets—the one thing it doesn't do is save your choices from session to session. If you find yourself modifying a format to the same custom settings over and over again, this tip is for you. Did you know that you can add your own custom format to the command? You will have to pop the hood on Dreamweaver's JavaScript engine, but don't worry; it's basically a copy-and-paste job.

To start, open the `tableFormats.js` file found in the Dreamweaver MX/Configuration/ Commands folder; this is where all the formats are stored. An entire format listing looks like this:

```
//Simple1
Formats[ ++i]  = new Array();          Formats[ i] .name=" Simple1";
Formats[ i] .firstRowColor="";         Formats[ i] .secondRowColor="";
Formats[ i] .topRowTextStyle=BOLD;     Formats[ i] .topRowAlign="";
Formats[ i] .topRowColor=" #99FF00";   Formats[ i] .topRowTextColor="";
Formats[ i] .leftColTextStyle=ITALIC;  Formats[ i] .leftColAlign="";
Formats[ i] .border=" 0";              Formats[ i] .rowLimit=" 0";
```

Copy one entire format and paste it above the first format, `Simple1`—that makes your entry the first in the dialog. Now make any changes you want to any of the property values. Probably the first change you should make is the name; I named mine "Krazy Kustom" (don't ask). If you want to have alternating row colors, change the `rowLimit` value to anything other than 0—make it 1 to have every other row alternate or 2 for every two rows. For text styles (`topRowTextStyle` and `leftColTextStyle`), use one of four constants: `NONE`, `BOLD`, `ITALIC`, or `BOLD_ITALIC`. For any other attribute, use an empty string ("") to tell Dreamweaver not to assign a value.

When you're done, save the JavaScript file and relaunch Dreamweaver. The next time you open Format Tables, you'll see your custom addition all nice and purty right there in the dialog—and you'll never have to customize again.

   DON'T BE A DRAG—NO, WAIT…DRAG ON!

I started out thinking this tip was going to be a warning about resizing table cells by dragging, but instead I'm happy to issue an all-clear signal! Used to be, in the old days (pre-Dreamweaver MX), that if you dragged the border of a cell to resize it, the values would suddenly appear in all the other cells of the table as well. This led to many a scrunched-up forehead as folks tried to figure out where those percentages or pixels came from—followed soon by the sound of gnashing teeth as the realization dawned that the table had to be reconstructed. Aarrgghhh!

Well, aarrgghhh no more, my friend. In Dreamweaver MX, you can now drag cell width or heights with impunity. Drag a cell width anywhere in the table and values are added to only the top row of cells. Increase a cell's height and only that cell's row is effected. It's a beautiful thing.

 ## AYE, AYE, CAPTION!

The move to create accessible websites has been extremely beneficial to a wide range of people. But even if you're not tasked with making your pages Section 508 compliant, you can spice up your tables—or at least make them more coherent— by using an accessibility-oriented tag, `<caption>`. The `<caption>...</caption>` tag pair is typically placed just after the opening `<table>` tag; by default, the caption (whatever is enclosed by the `<caption>` tag) appears above the table, but you can display it underneath by changing the `align` attribute to `bottom`.

So what's the best way to add a caption to a table in Dreamweaver? If it's something you want to add consistently, go to Edit > Preferences and, in the Accessibility category, choose the Tables option. After you insert a table normally, the Accessibility Options for Tables dialog is displayed and you can enter your caption text there and choose an alignment (top, bottom, left, or right). If you're an off-and-on caption addict, go into Code view and drag-and-drop the Caption object from the Tables category of the Insert bar immediately following the opening `<table>` tag within the table structure. Then add your text and set the attributes by hand or use the Tag inspector with the `<caption>` tag selected.

 ## KEEPING TO THE RATIO

When are images like tables? When you resize them by dragging. Select a table and you'll notice the same configuration of sizing handles you see when you choose an image. You can drag these table sizing handles the same way you can with an image— including the trick of keeping the same width-to-height ratio. Begin dragging a table by its corner and then press Shift; the table will snap to the closest match of the original width-height ratio. Resize the table the way you want it and release the mouse and then the Shift key. Presto—your table is made proportionately larger or smaller.

CHAPTER 3 • The Best Table Tips   **57**

   BATTEN DOWN THE HATCHES

Watch out—there's a big ole storm of nasty browsers heading your way. If your table structure is not locked down tight, they might blow it out of the water. Some of the earlier browsers had a bad habit of adjusting cell widths and heights willy nilly; if you've ever seen an exploded table, you know it's not a pretty sight. What's a poor table builder supposed to do?

Let's borrow a technique from our brethren in the web tool biz, the graphics editors. When you slice up an image in an program like Fireworks or Photoshop and export it, the graphic becomes a table of images. Holding the table tightly together is an additional row and another column, filled with a transparent single pixel GIF image. The GIFs, often called *shims* or *spacers* when used like this, are set to a specific width across the top of the table, which correspond to the column width; the same method sets the height of the spacers to the row heights. Together the added row and column make it impossible to break apart the table structure. So where do you get these marvelous wee beasties? If you've imported any sliced graphics into your site, you probably already have them. Look for spacer.gif or shim.gif in the Assets panel.

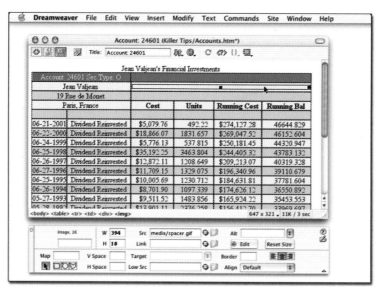

NESTING MADE SIMPLE

What's the key guideline to building complex tables? When in doubt, nest. Putting one table inside another, which is also known as *nesting tables*, makes tables more stable and, at the same time, more flexible. The alternative—merging and splitting cells— leads to really messy code that's not only more difficult to decipher (and thus modify), but also makes the table flimsier and more prone to collapse.

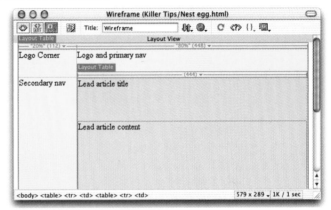

Let's say you've put together a two-column layout table with the navigation on the left and the content on the right. In many cases, your main content cell is going to be subdivided in some way to make the text more readable and the design more pleasing. Rather than try to split the content cell into two or more columns and then split one of those columns into two rows, just drop in a one-row, two-column table. Then, in one of the columns, plop down another nested table with a single column and two rows. Think onesies and twosies when you're adding nested tables—keep the interior tables fairly simple for the most flexible structures.

   SORT AND FORMAT OR FORMAT AND SORT?

Sort Table and Format Table are real powerhouses when it comes to managing your tabular data; you'll find them both under the Commands menu. But if you need a formatted, sorted table, which command do you run first? And the answer is that word you love to hate, "Depends." You can apply formatting to table elements two ways: the formatting attributes are either coded within each table row tag, `<tr>`, or within every table cell, `<td>`. If you'd rather use the `<tr>` method, which offers cleaner code, sort before you format. On the other hand, if you want to go the `<td>`

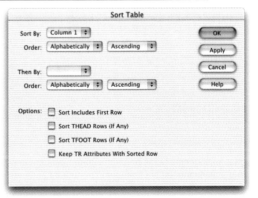

route for more granular control, format first and sort later. Opting for the second technique? Be sure to select the Apply All Attributes to TD Tags Instead of TR Tags option in the Format Table dialog.

   THE BEST OF BOTH WORLDS: SET AND EXPANDING COLUMNS

This one's a classic, but I figure there are enough young'uns out there that it's still worth the paper it's printed on (and this glossy stuff don't come cheap). One of the basic challenges of using tables for layout is trying to make the content resize to the width of the browser window while keeping other areas from expanding. Let's assume your navigation is on the left and your content is on the right— hey, there's a novel idea!

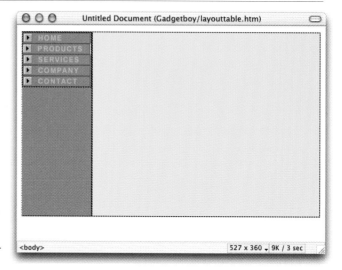

Start out with a two-column, three-row table at 100%. Set borders, cell spacing, and cell padding all to 0. Set the left column to the width of your navigation elements either by dragging the border or selecting the top cell and entering the pixel value in the Width field of the Property inspector. Notice that I said *pixel* value; you want the set column to use a hard value, not a percentage. Now you

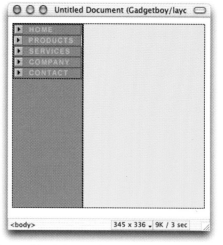

can fill those columns to the brim and look forward to hours of fun resizing that browser window.

IMPORTING STRUCTURED DATA

Dreamweaver has a cool command that allows you to bring in data from a spreadsheet or database program. All you need do is output the data in the proper format. Great, but what's the proper format? Dreamweaver's File > Import > Tablular Data feature is pretty flexible and can work with almost any kind of text file where the data is separated or delimited by a certain character. Typically, you're trying to bring in data from either a spreadsheet program like Microsoft Excel or a database program like Microsoft Access. Just to keep life interesting, these two programs use different commands to do the same thing. Here's a little help to get your data moving on the right track from those programs into Dreamweaver.

From Access, begin by selecting a table or query before choosing File > Export and then set the Save As Type option to Text. Clear the Save Formatted checkbox. When you click Save, the Export Text Wizard appears. Although there are many ways to go, the best combo I've found is to choose Delimited on the first step and then select Comma as the delimiting character, with Quotes as the Text Qualifier. (If your data has quotation marks in it, choose Tab as a delimiter and None as the Text Qualifier).

From Excel, select File > Save As and choose either Text (Tab-delimited) or CSV (Comma-delimited). Again, the decision depends on what's in your data—for the most part, I go with the tab-delimited files. Whichever you choose, make sure that Dreamweaver is set to use the corresponding delimiter in the Import Tabular Data dialog, or you're in for a heap of clean up.

BRINGING TABLE EDITING UP TO SPEED

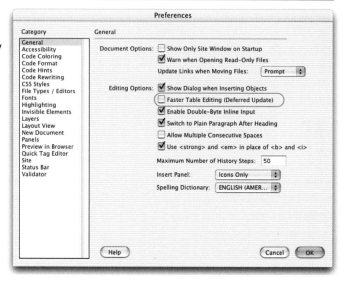

When Dreamweaver 1.0 was first introduced, it was a cutting edge tool in many ways, but table editing was not one of them. Adding content to a table cell could be described only as glacial. To correct this problem in the short-term, Dreamweaver 1.2 introduced a new preference option: Faster Table Editing (Deferred Update) in the General category of Preferences. When this option was selected, Dreamweaver would expand the table vertically as you added content, but would not adjust the horizontal cell widths until you either clicked outside the table or pressed a keyboard shortcut, Ctrl+spacebar (Command+spacebar).

In the subsequent versions, Dreamweaver radically improved its editing speed and now it is almost impossible to type faster than Dreamweaver can render. On a good day, I can get up to 115 wpm and I still can't outpace Dreamweaver's table editing. The Faster Table Editing option is still in Preferences, however, and it's turned on by default. If you're ready to experience real-time table editing, do yourself a favor and clear that option.

TABLE WIDTHS ON A NEED-TO-KNOW BASIS

The first time you insert a table, Dreamweaver displays a preset width value of 75%; you also can set the width in pixels if you prefer. What many people don't grasp is that you don't have to declare a table width at all, and in many cases it is better not to. Don't misunderstand me; I'm not advocating that you eliminate the width value when you create your table—if you do that, you'll get an impossibly skinny table that you're going to have to expand to insert your content. No, the way to do it is to keep the table at whatever width you are comfortable with as you add your text, images, and what-have-you. When you're done, select the Clear Column Widths button on the Table Property inspector (it's the top left in the group of six buttons). Now the information is free to flow and the table cells will be only as wide the content needs them to be.

ADD A ROW, ADD A COLUMN

After carefully, meticulously, crafting your table of facts and figures and getting it just right, word comes down that you have to add another column at the end and another row in the middle. No problem—you've got a couple of routes to take that will lead you over this particular molehill. Adding columns to the outside right of a table is pretty straightforward; all you need to do is increase the number of columns in the Table Property inspector. The same method is true if you want to add one or more rows to the bottom of the table.

If, however, your additional column needs to be on the left of the table, you need to go the menu route. Position your cursor anywhere in the first column and choose Modify > Table > Insert Column. Similarly, if you have to place a new row on top of the table, set the cursor in a top row cell and select Modify > Table > Insert Row. Both menu options are available from the context menu as well. If you find that you need to add multiple rows or columns to the outside, select the Insert Rows or Columns menu item.

To insert a column in the middle of a table, place your cursor to the right of the place where you want the new column to appear before you choose Insert Column. For interior rows, put the cursor in a cell beneath the row-to-be and select Insert Row. Alternatively, you could use the Insert Rows or Columns dialog.

   MOVING CELLS AND CELL CONTENTS

Need to relocate that cellular matter? You can move entire rows or columns simply by cutting and pasting. Rows will appear above the current cursor position and columns will appear to the left. So how do you move a row or column to the outside? Add a temporary column or row using one of the techniques outlined in the previous tip. Then, place your cursor in the newly created column or row and paste away. The content will show up next to the cursor and now you're free to delete your temporary column or row.

I'LL TAKE THE MEAT; HOLD THE BUN

Select any cell, row, or column and do a quick copy-and-paste: what do you get? Pretty much everything—the content as well as the surrounding tags and all of their attributes. But what if you want to move only the content? The copy portion of the formula is the same; however, instead of a standard paste (Ctrl+V or Command+V), use the Paste HTML command (Ctrl+Shift+V or Command+Shift+V). Whatever was in the cell you copied is added to whatever is in the cell you're pasting to. If you're pasting into a Dreamweaver-style empty cell held open with a non-breaking space, the ` ` entity is replaced by the incoming content.

LAURA ZOLOFT, TAB HUNTER

Those nifty little tabs shown in Layout view can be quite a boon when you're trying to uncover the inner secrets of deeply nested tables (see "Switch Hitter: Going from Standard to Layout View" in this chapter). They're even great for quickly gleaning column widths. True, you can make the identifying tabs disappear by switching to Standard view; so what if you want to work in Layout view without the tabs mucking up your view? Even choosing Hide All Visual Aids from the Toolbar's View Options menu won't cut it. Your answer lies in the menus: View > Table View > Show Layout Table Tabs, to be precise. This command is a toggle, so select it again to turn those tabs back on.

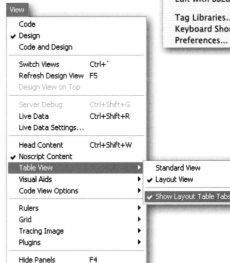

  SNAP GOES THE MOUSE

Drawing cells and tables in Layout view is quite literally a snap. To make it easy to create coherent structures, Dreamweaver defaults to snapping new cell and table borders to those already on the page. Just get within eight pixels of an existing edge and—SNAP!—you're locked into position. That's all well and good for most designs, but suppose that you wanted to draw out a cell not exactly touching its neighbor? To temporarily override the snapping border, hold down the Alt (Option) key while drawing a layout cell. To contemporaneously ride a snapping turtle—you're on your own.

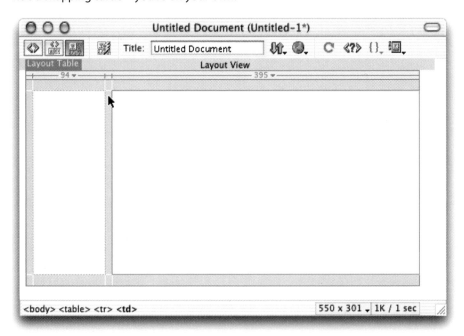

SWITCH HITTER: GOING FROM STANDARD TO LAYOUT VIEW

One of my favorite teaching tricks—I could try to pass it off as a shining example of hard-earned knowledge, but it's still a trick—is used to demonstrate nested table structure. What is close to incomprehensible in standard view, especially if you're looking at a table design you didn't build yourself, becomes as clear as the bottled water of your choice in Layout view. There are a couple of ways to switch between the two views: Choose View > Table View and then select either Standard View or Layout View, or from the Layout category of the Insert bar, click the Standard View or Layout View button.

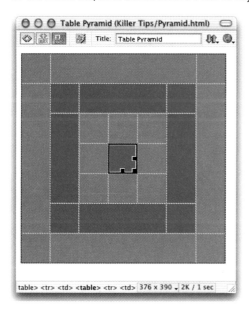 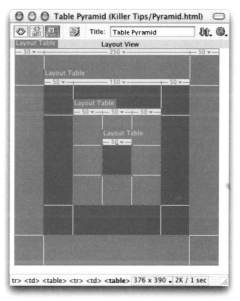

THE VAST EMPTINESS OF WAYOUT, LAYOUT SPACE

As pointed out in the previous tip, looking at your tables in both Standard and Layout view is free and easy. But suppose that you want to add some content to the table while in Layout view—now *that's* gonna cost you. OK, the tariff isn't that high—any cells with content already in them can be added to or modified at no extra charge. Totally empty cells or cells with just a non-breaking space in them, however; well, that's another matter. Layout view sees such blank cells as just structural and not load-bearing, if you will. To insert text, graphics, or any other content into an empty cell in Layout view, you need to explicitly draw the cell. Dreamweaver helps by snapping to the edges of existing cells, but you still need to push that mouse around to make it happen.

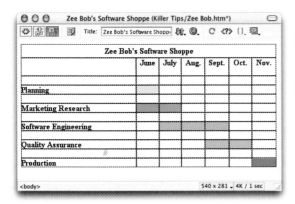

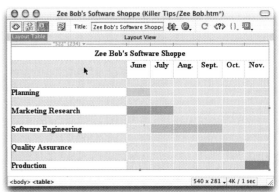

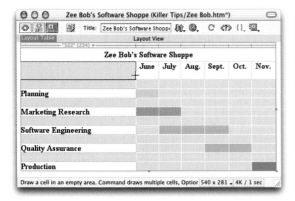

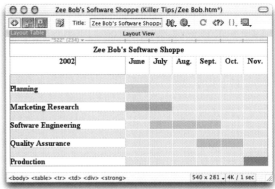

THE PLAGUE OF EMPTY CELLS

When Layout view was first introduced, Dreamweaver had a number of what are euphemistically called "issues." But why toy with euphemisms? There were bugs, *bugs*, I say! Chief among them was the tendency for structural layout cells (automatically created cells) to be totally empty. Without the benefit of a non-breaking space, such tables were very fragile and prone to collapse. Dreamweaver MX fixed the basic problem; now, when you are drawing layout cells,   codes are automatically inserted. Like a meddling neighbor watching a friend paint a room, however, I've got to say, "Missed a spot!" Resize a table in Layout view by dragging its border and some of the non-breaking spaces disappear. To avoid the loss of these precious   codes—and save yourself the work of putting them back in—resize the table via the Property inspector.

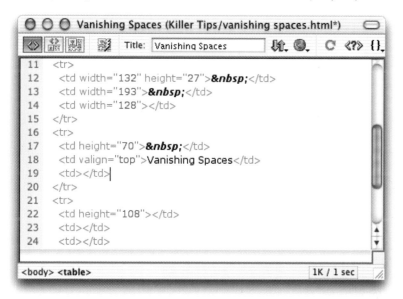

  LAYOUT CELL PROPERTIES

You may notice that the Property inspector for layout tables and cells is quite lean and mean. You have far fewer attributes and options available than when you select a similar tag in Standard view. To add such attributes—like a background image—you have two options. One way is to select the cell, switch to Standard view, and then make your choices from the full-service Property inspector. Another way is to select the cell and then go to the new Tag Inspector, found in the Code panel group. The cell won't highlight in the tree view, but all its available properties are primed and ready to go.

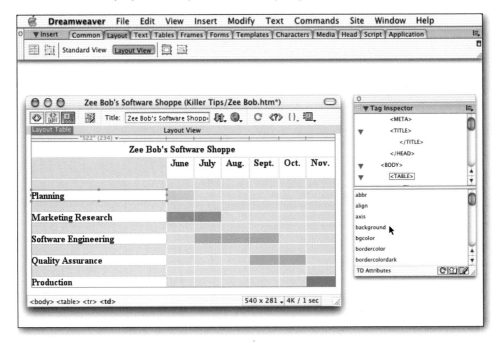

⬤ ⬤ ⬤ **THIS TIP TOTALLY RULES**

Sometimes it is helpful to separate multiple column content in the same table with a straight line or rule. I can think of a couple of ways to fulfill this wish right off the bat. Generally, I start by making sure that the content rows I want to separate have at least one row between them—call this the *rule row*. Select rule row and merge all the cells into one. Now you have the choice of inserting a horizontal rule tag, `<hr>`, or a small colored GIF (like 2 pixels x 2 pixels). Change the width of either to 100% and, as they say in pseudo-France, *woilah*.

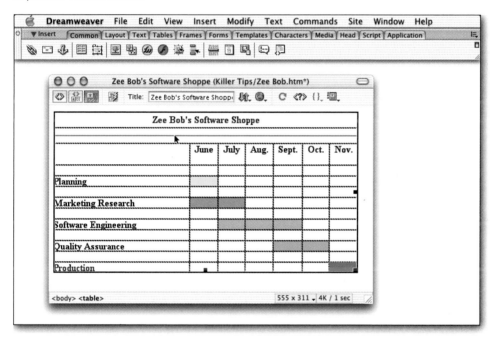

 CALLING ALL BORDERS

Creating a bordered text box in CSS is pretty easy, but if you can't use CSS on your site (sob!), there's a way to get the same effect with tables (yay!). The trick is to nest one table inside another where the outer table has both a background color (that becomes your border) and a small amount of cell padding (which translates into the border width). The inner table is set to 100% width, a larger cell padding value, to keep it away from the outer border, and given its own background color. The interesting thing about using this technique to create a border is that no border attributes are used—or rather, they are specifically not used and set to zero—for both tables. Here's some sample code to gnaw on:

```html
<table width="250" border="0" cellpadding="1" cellspacing="0"
bgcolor="#000000" >
  <tr>
    <td> <table width="100%" border="0" cellspacing="0" cellpadding="20"
    bgcolor="white">
        <tr>
          <td bgcolor="#FFFF99" align="left" valign="top">
            <h3 align="center">HoJo's Tip Of the Day</h3>
            <p>Cross-browser bordered tables are the cat's meow.</p>
            </td>
        </tr>
      </table>
      </td>
  </tr>
</table>
```

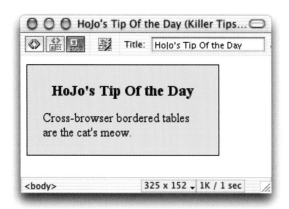

ACCESSIBLE STYLISH HEADERS

As mentioned in an earlier tip ("Aye, Aye Caption!"), setting the Tables checkbox in the Accessibility category of Preferences brings up an additional dialog when you are inserting a table. One of the options is to specify a header row, column, or both. Choose one of these selections and Dreamweaver converts the corresponding <td> tags to <th> tags. This action is taken to comply with §1194.22(g) of Section 508.

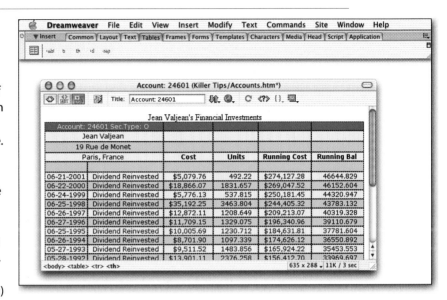

Browsers typically render <th> tags as bold and centered, which may or may not be the look you're going for. Using CSS, you can style the <th> tags however you like and still stay within compliance. Screen readers react to the tag itself, not the way that it is rendered.

   ## YOUR PAD IS MY SPACE; MY SPACE IS YOUR PAD

Do you ever find yourself unable to remember the simplest things? No? Okay, then skip this tip—you're obviously too good for it. For me, I can't seem to remember the difference between cell padding and cell spacing. One controls the number of pixels between cells and one is the margin within the cells—but which is which?

By default, Dreamweaver leaves both these values blank when you first insert a table. Of course, not having a value doesn't mean the browser doesn't use any padding or spacing. Browsers display 2 pixels for both values if you don't specify a number. For a table full of structured data, I like to use rows with alternating background colors—which requires a 0 border and no room between the cells. (Otherwise, the background of the document will show through and break up the solid row background color.) Okay, so, in the Property inspector, I set the border to 0, but which of the two—cell padding or cell spacing—do I zero out? Here's my memory trick: I know I've got to set the Border to 0, and who is Border's good buddy, hanging out just to his left? Why it's old CellSpace! So, I set CellSpace to 0 also and I'm solid—and so is my background color.

Speed Daemons

Watch Out for Falling Browsers

We all know what a drag it is to make pages that look good in older browsers like Netscape 4.x. To make your site look the same in older browsers and modern

Speed Daemons
browser compatibility tips

ones, you often must sacrifice the appearance of the site. Bear in mind that it is rare that someone—other than web developers or clients—will see your page in both older and newer browsers. Typically, the general public uses only one browser or another and will never compare a site between browsers. All that really matters is that the site looks acceptable and is fully functional in the browsers of your target audience. Read the last few sentences over and over again until you've committed them to memory. You'll be better for it, and you won't consider wasting precious time making every last detail the same between browsers.

Everything you'll find in this chapter relates to browsers in some way, shape, or form. Not only do you learn cool tips for Dreamweaver, but you also learn general browser usage tips that will speed up workflow and make you a better all-around developer. You'll get solutions to tough issues specific to certain browsers, fun things you can do for some browsers, and a bunch of ideas you never considered before.

EDIT BROWSER LIST

Previewing pages early and often in various browsers will save you the cost of headache medicine. To make this agonizing process a bit less painful, set up additional browsers for Dreamweaver to use with its Preview in Browser feature. Select Edit > Preferences (Dreamweaver > Preferences on Mac OS X) or Ctrl+U (Command+U) and then click Preview in Browser from the category list on the left. Click the Add (+) button to reveal the Add Browser dialog. Don't give the browser a name just yet, or when you do the next step the value in the Name field will be replaced. Instead, browse to the executable file for your installed browser. Next, give the browser a meaningful, friendly name. This is the name that will appear in the menu. Lastly, decide whether you want this to be the primary browser accessed by the keyboard shortcut F12, the secondary browser accessed by Shift+F12 or neither. You don't have to make it primary or secondary, if you'd rather access the browser from the menu File > Preview in Browser submenu. By the way, Windows users, you can install as many Netscape browsers as your machine can tolerate, but you can have only one Internet Explorer.

FASHIONING FURRY, FRIENDLY FAVICONS

Fav-i-*huhs*? You may not know what they're called, but I know you've seen 'em. Bookmark a site as a favorite in Internet Explorer 4 and up, and often you'll see a small custom logo in place of the standard program icon in the Favorites list. That's a *favicon*—and you can insert the necessary code right in Dreamweaver. You'll need to create the graphic separately, of course; you'll find

all the tools you need at www.favicon.com. After you've fashioned your fabulous favicon, put a `<link>` tag in the `<head>` section of your doc, like this:

```
<LINK REL="SHORTCUT ICON" HREF="/images/bigco.ico">
```

The `rel` attribute needs to read "shortcut icon" but `href` can point to whatever .ico file you've created. When you upload your file, if you let Dreamweaver put the dependent files, your favicon will be copied automagically.

   CLOSE THAT WINDOW!

Closing a popup window with a link is done with a simple piece of JavaScript code. Don't start sweating yet; when I say simple code, I really mean it. Just select the text or image that you want to use as a link to close the window, and then in the Link field of the Property inspector, enter the following code:

```
javascript:self.close();
```

You can even apply this method to a form button by using `self.close()` as the value of an onClick attribute, like in the tip "Button, Button, Who's Got the Button?" in Chapter 7.

GET OUT OF GEE-AOL

Bit o' British humour, eh wot? Although AOL may not be expanding at the phenomenal rate
it once was, the service still has a tremendous number of members who browse the web—
and if your site is accessible on the web, you need to make sure it looks okay on AOL. Since
version 3, AOL has relied on the installed copy of Internet Explorer as its external browser
for Windows systems. The latest version of AOL for the Mac, however, uses the Netscape
Gecko engine. All browsers, though, are subject to the service's graphics compression.
To be sure all of your AOL dots are connected, visit the AOL Webmaster site,
http://webmaster.info.aol.com.

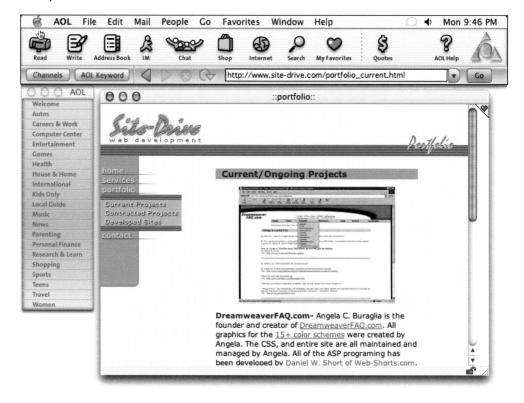

<HEAD> 'EM OFF

Dreamweaver includes a pretty flexible behavior called Check Browser that stays on the current page or redirects the user to a different page, depending on the browser version. When you apply the Check Browser behavior, it is triggered by the onLoad event of the <body> tag; in other words, after the page has finished loading, the JavaScript code checks the browser and redirects the page according to your settings.

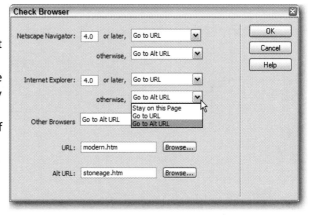

This is all well and good if one of your options is to stay on the same page—but what if you've got two separate pages you're redirecting to? With the standard Dreamweaver implementation, the page has to load before it redirects; even if the page is blank, you may get a little flash of the page before the redirection kicks in. The way around this is to move the function call that Dreamweaver inserted in the <body> tag up to the <head>. To do this, locate the onLoad event in the <body> tag; it'll look something like this:

```
<body onLoad="MM_checkBrowser(4.0,1,2,4.0,0,2,2,'main.htm','altmain.htm');
➥return document.MM_returnValue">
```

Copy the bolded code from your own <body> tag and paste it within the <script> tag in the <head>, just above the line that starts with function MM_checkBrowser. You'll also need to delete the complete the entire onLoad event in the <body> tag. Now, just like with a server-side redirection script, the redirection takes place in the blink of an eye—without the flash of a page.

ALRIGHT, NETSCAPE 4.X, HUG THOSE MARGINS, BUDDY!

So, you're cool, you're hip, you're savvy—you nod knowingly when fellow web designers mention "the @ Import trick" (if you don't, sneak over to Chapter 2, quick like a bunny)—but what do you put in those style sheets intended for only Netscape 4.x? One of the headache-inducing Netscape 4.x issues is how it handles page

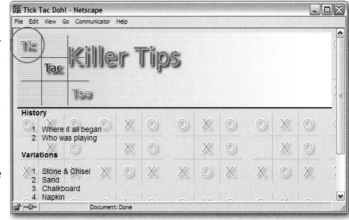

margins. With Internet Explorer 4+ or Netscape 6 and greater, use CSS to set the `<body>` margins to 0 and you're done; with earlier versions of Netscape, it's hoop jumping time. First, in the Netscape-specific style sheet—the one you link, not import—set the top and left margins to –10. Yes, that's negative 10. Why? Don't ask. Next, in the Page Properties dialog (Modify > Page Properties), set Margin Width and Margin Height both to 0. With both the CSS and HTML specifications in place, Netscape 4.x margins are as snug as a bug in a rug.

TO PARENS OR NOT TO PARENS

Dreamweaver newbies applying their first behavior are faced with a mind-twisting choice—make the wrong move and you're cutting off your browser backward compatibility. For example, suppose that you're applying a Show-Hide Layer behavior to an image and you want the behavior to fire when the user rolls over an image—so you pick onMouseOver from the Events listing, right? But what about that other choice: (onMouseOver)? What's the difference and what's the

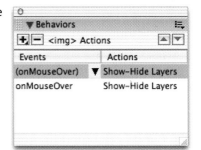

best choice? You'll see the parenthetical choices when your Show Event For options is pointed to Internet Explorer 4.0 – 6.0 or Netscape 6.0. Choose the event without the parentheses and the behavior is applied to the `<img>` tag itself. That's okay—if you don't care about your rollover working in Netscape 4.x browsers. Select the event in parentheses, however, and you're covered all the way; the behavior is applied to an automatically added `<a>` tag and that works in all fourth generation browsers and above.

TILE NO MORE!

You can create some pretty cool designs by placing an image in the background of a table—but that's an iffy proposition in Netscape 4.x. What happens with background images in that oh-so-troubled browser? The browser takes whatever is in the background of the first cell in the top row and repeats it in every cell—nice, eh? To get the effect you want—of the entire image appearing behind the table, not just the one small part—you'll need to nest the multiple-cell table in a single-cell table. The single-cell table should have your background image and the multiple-cell table should have a transparent GIF in the `<table>` background. I don't know why it works and I don't really care—and after you finally get the effect you want, cross-browser, neither will you.

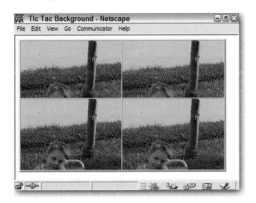

 ## QUIT MAKING ME QUIRKY!

You're familiar with doctype switching, right? This is the way that modern, version 6 and later browsers render the page in a strict standards-based compliance mode or in a looser, so-called quirks mode, depending on the document type declared. Seems like there's another wrinkle for those designers creating XHTML-compliant pages. Dreamweaver, rightfully, includes the XML encoding declaration at the top of every XHTML page. Unfortunately, this throws Internet Explorer 6 into quirks mode, which causes the page to render differently than it should. The sad-but-true solution is to remove the XML declaration—a case of Dreamweaver being a little too far ahead of the curve.

   BROWSER CHECKING WITHOUT THE BROWSER

There's what, a *gazillion* browser versions in use on the web now? Oh, wait, I forgot about the latest release—make that a gazillion and one. How do you check your pages against them all when you can't possibly have all the browsers? Dreamweaver's Target Browser Check is one often over-looked alternative that gives you a way to check your entire site

against 16 major browser versions. To see the possibilities, choose Window > Results > Target Browser Check and then select the green arrow to get started. Selecting all the browser versions in the Target Browser Check will definitely lead you to say, "Well, you can't please all the people all the time," unless your page is just bare text. It's best to decide which browsers you intend to support and just run Target Browser Check against them. I, for example, rarely check for anything below a version 4 browser these days—it all depends on the client's web statistics. If the logs show that 15 percent of the site's visitors are using Netscape 2.0, I'm going to be sure the site looks acceptable in that browser.

   PREPARING TO GO TO THE TABLE(S)

If you're faced with transforming a site that is compatible with fourth genera-tion browsers to one readable by earlier versions, one option is to convert your layers to tables. The Modify > Convert > Layers to Table command does this in a snap—but you've got to do your prep work first. For best results, make sure that all of your content on the page is in a layer; otherwise, Dreamweaver

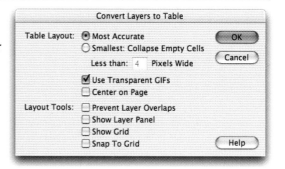

moves the content not inside a layer to the bottom of the page. Not pretty. Second, see that no layers overlap or else the command stops and yells at you. Third, nested layers are a no-no. Finally, the `<ilayer>`, as nifty as it is, is not supported by Dreamweaver, so you'll need to change those tags to either `<span>` or `<div>`.

  LAYING DOWN A LAYER

The previous tip talked about the joys of converting from layers to tables—well, what if you're going the other way? Again, Dreamweaver's Modify > Convert > Tables to Layers command is pretty thorough; if anything, it's a little too thorough. Every object in the `<body>`, regardless of whether it is in a table, gets placed into a layer. Want another example of such pedal-to-the-metal efficiency? Every content-filled (or background-using) cell within a table is put into a separate layer—convert a page with a 3×5 table and we're talking 15 layers. Bottom line: use Convert Tables to Layers judiciously.

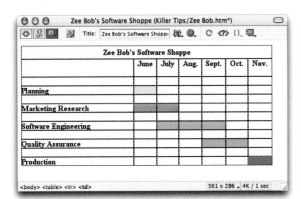 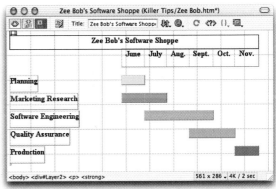

   RIGHT MARGIN ANOMALY

You've given a table 100 percent width, yet when you look at it in Internet Explorer 5.5+ the table fills all but about 10 pixels to the left of the space reserved for the scrollbar even though you've set your margins in the `<body>` tag to zero. Assuming that something is wrong with the browser (which there is; it is a bug)
you decide to refresh. What a relief—the little right margin is gone now. It isn't until you've closed the browser or cleared your cache that you encounter the anomaly again. We certainly can't expect visitors to refresh the page just to see it correctly, and we don't want to force a refresh because that just isn't elegant. Don't ask me why using at least one of these three solutions solves the problem; there is no logical explanation. You can either use an external JavaScript file, link to a Favicon (see "Fashioning Furry, Friendly Favicons" earlier in this chapter), or my personal favorite: link to an external CSS file. Of course, if you use embedded CSS to declare your margins, you won't run into this little bugger either.

   PLACEMENT, PLACEMENT, PLACEMENT

Well, it's not exactly location, location, location, but when it comes to backward compatibility with layers, it's the next best thing. If you've ever looked at a layer-based page in a browser that is not layer capable, you know that you can get into a big mess in a big hurry. There is, however, a technique that gives you the best possible solution for both layer and non-layer browser worlds—and that's placement. The earlier browsers don't under-stand the `<div>` tag and so it's totally ignored; as I'm sure you know, `<div>` tags are used by Dreamweaver to create layers by default. They do, however, understand and render the content within those tags. It's good practice to place your `<div>` tags in the HTML document in the order in which they should appear: for example, the heading area should go above the content which should, in turn, go above the footer. Dreamweaver inserts the code, depending on the cursor placement. Not only does proper contextual placement help backward browser compatibility, it also is a forward-thinking requirement for accessibility. How do you re-order your `<div>` tags? Although you could cut-and-paste the code, I prefer to drag the layer icons (seen while Invisible Elements is enabled) into place.

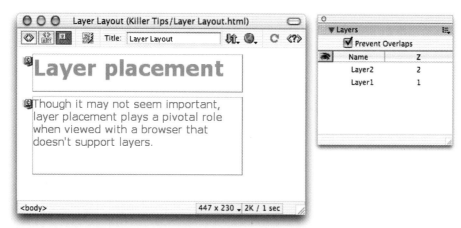

DHTML BACKWARD COMPATIBILITY

So you've got this nifty Dynamic HTML animation that you've been up weeks tweaking to get it just right and suddenly you find out the client's Big Cheese just can't give up his 3.0 browser. Your options are these: (a) jump out the nearest window (luckily you're on the first floor, so it's just symbolic gesture); (b) break-in and upgrade the Big Cheese's browser (a little B-and-E is generally not good for one's resume); or (c) make the DHTML animation backward compatible. Although there's no way your animation is going to fly around a third-generation browser screen like it does in fourth generation and later browsers, you can maintain a semblance of similarity to your design. The trick is to begin and end your DHTML animation in the same spot. Luckily, because you're using Dreamweaver's Timelines panel to create your DHTML movement anyway, this is pretty simple to do. If this is work-able for your design, you're good to go. If not, well, that window's looking pretty inviting…

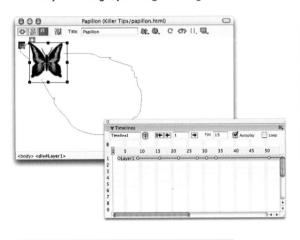

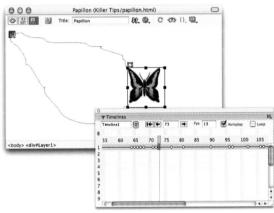

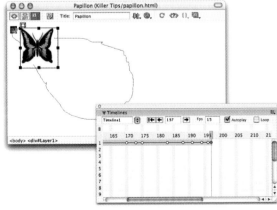

 PREVIEWING ROOT RELATIVE LINKS LOCALLY

Working with site root relative links? Did you know that Dreamweaver manages a little slight of hand that makes it possible to preview pages with site root relative links (up to a point, anyway)? As I'm sure you know, document relative links preview just fine in Dreamweaver. Dreamweaver creates the temporary file it actually sends to the browser in the same folder as the current page being previewed—so document relative links are a snap. Site root relative links are a different story, however. Let's say that you're working on a page that is saved in a folder three levels deep in your site and you have a `<img>` tag with a `src` set to `/assets/images/logo.gif`. How does Dreamweaver's Preview in Browser (which is just working with the local file system, not an actual http-type URL) know where to get the image? If you look at the source when previewing, you'll see that Dreamweaver actually converts the site root relative link to a document relative one. This means that the image `src` in this example would become `../../assets/images/logo.gif`. This works swell for the first page, but if you want to check links from that page, you're better off previewing through a server—either local or remote. Why? Dreamweaver's bit of legerdemain extends only to the first page previewed; any site root relative links on a second page go untranslated.

 SASSY STATUS BAR

Way down in the lower left of the browser window lives the status bar. Usually, the status bar provides helpful info, such as the progress of the loading page or the URL of the hyperlink the pointer is over. My favorite use of the status bar is to provide a copyright message when the user's pointer is over an image. Dreamweaver makes doing status bar messages easy with the Set Text of Status Bar behavior. First make the image a link, be it real or null (see "Watch Out for Killer Octothorpes" in Chapter 7), and then click the Add (+) button on the Behaviors panel and choose Set Text > Set Text of Status Bar. When the dialog appears, type **You Taka My Stuff, I Breaka Your Face** or another appropri-

ate message, and then click OK. Make sure that you've chosen the appropriate event in the Behaviors panel. In our case, we want (onMouseOver) in parentheses. (See "To Parens or Not to Parens" earlier in this chapter for more info.) If you want the message to disappear when the pointer moves off the image, apply the behavior a second time, but don't add a message; just click OK. Don't forget to set the event to (onMouseOut).

SNAPPY BROWSER SIZING

It sure is handy to have the ability to
resize a browser window when you
are doing site testing. Just a simple
snippet of JavaScript can resize most
any browser window. The `resizeTo()`
function lets you specify a width
and height argument that will snap
the current browser window to the
specified width and height values.
Let's create a page in Dreamweaver that

you will view in the browser to later make into a browser "favorite." Click the Hyperlink
object found in the common category of the Insert bar. In the Text field, enter the text you
want your Favorites/Bookmarks to display. I've used **Resize to 800x600**. In the Link field,
type **javascript:resizeTo(800,600);** and then click OK. Now view the page in a browser.
Right-click (Ctrl+click) the hyperlink and select either Add to Favorites or Add Bookmark (or
a similar command) from the context menu. If you are prompted that what you are adding
may not be safe, confirm that it is ok to add it. Some browsers will even let you click and
drag the link into the browser toolbar so that the function is available as a button. Now
whenever you want to resize a browser, just choose the favorite you created.

   ## GO BACK THREE SPACES

Let's say that you've spawned a new
browser window that for some (hopefully
good) reason does not include the
browser's toolbar. Now your users are
left without their friend the Back button.
You can emulate the browser's Back
button functionality with the following
JavaScript added to the Link field of the
Property inspector:

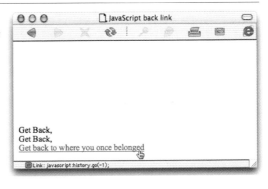

```
javascript:history.go(-1);
```

The function will accept both negative and positive values so that you can use it to move
back or ahead as many pages as you like, provided that the user has visited the pages
already so that they're in the browser's history.

   ELIMINATE THE INTERNET EXPLORER 6 IMAGE TOOLBAR

Surf the Internet using Internet Explorer 6 and sooner or later you'll get a glimpse of the Image toolbar. Usually an image that is equal to or over 200px by 200px is required to make the Image toolbar appear, but there are other factors which can allow for it to be shown on images as small as 124px by 124px. I try not to worry about what will or will not make the Image toolbar appear and just add the `<meta>` tag needed to turn it off. In the Head category of the Insert bar, click the Meta object. Select the HTTP-equivalent from the Attributes drop-down list, type **imagetoolbar** in the Value field, type **no** in the Content field, and then click OK. You also can handle the Image toolbar on a case-by-case basis by adding the `galleryimg` attribute to the `<img>` tag with a value of `no`, using the Tag inspector or via Code view.

   COLOR CATCHER

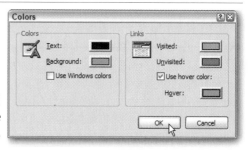

Back in the days of Dreamweaver 4, a new document had a color defined for text and the background color in the `<body>` tag. In an effort to be standards compliant, the `<body>` tag does not contain any attributes in Dreamweaver MX by default. On one hand this is great, because you don't have to waste your time stripping out the deprecated code, but on the other hand it can also mean that colors get accidentally forgotten. Here's a great way to keep on top of not only text and background color but also hyperlink colors. Using any Internet Explorer 5 or higher, select Tools > Internet Options and then click the Colors button near the bottom of the dialog. Uncheck the Use Windows Colors box and then click the color buttons so that you can choose some really obnoxious colors as the default. Whenever you see the obnoxious color while viewing a page in the browser, you'll know that colors were not explicitly specified. You can then correct your page by adding the appropriate CSS and chuckle knowingly when it isn't your page.

OPEN A WINDOW

There comes a time in every developer's life when you
need to have a null hyperlink (see "Watch Out for Killer
Octothorpes" in Chapter 7) that triggers another browser
window to open. When browser size doesn't matter,
selecting the `_blank` option in the Target field of the
Property inspector (which adds `target="_blank"` to
the `<a>` tag) is the easiest way to open a new browser
window. When you need more functionality than a simple
target attribute, you can use the Open Browser Window
behavior. You can specify the width and height of the
window and include other browser attributes if you like.
Let me rephrase that; you *should* specify the width and
height of the window or check at least one attribute.
If you don't, some browsers will display attributes even
though you have not

checked any of the attributes. If for some reason I
don't want to specify width
and height, I check off all
options and modify the
source code from `yes` to `no`
where appropriate, and that
takes care of things. Like
anything else you do for
the web, test it out.

Occasionally you may have several hyperlinks on the page you want to open in a new
window of the same size and attributes, but you don't necessarily want each hyperlink to
spawn a new window of its own. Each hyperlink can share the same new window if you
assign the same Window Name value each time you apply the behavior.

 MAKE DREAMWEAVER THE DEFAULT EDITOR

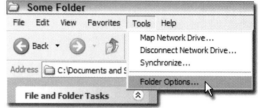

One of the best ways to learn is to examine existing pages on the web. Internet Explorer offers an Edit button on its toolbar that will open the current page in the editor selected. I've tested this tip out in IE 5.5 on Windows 2000 and IE 6 on Windows XP. If you're using another Windows operating system or Internet Explorer version, this may or may not work. That said, let's make Dreamweaver available as the default editor for Internet Explorer. First you'll need to open any folder on your system in Windows Explorer, and then choose Tools > Folder Options. Click the File Types tab and then select HTML from the list of Registered File Types. Now click the Advanced button. Click Edit in the list of Actions and then click the Edit button. In the Application used to perform action field, browse the Dreamweaver MX executable file. Whatever appears in that field must include quotations around the path, followed by %1 so that it looks something like this:

```
"C:\Program Files\Macromedia\Dreamweaver MX\Dreamweaver.exe" %1
```

Now launch Internet Explorer if it isn't open already, and choose Tools > Internet Options and select the Programs tab. Assuming that all went well in the previous steps, you should be able to select Dreamweaver MX from the HTML editor drop-down list and click OK. Now the Edit button on the toolbar should open the current page in Dreamweaver MX so that you can examine or edit the code.

● **FOCUS POCUS**

Those focus lines that appear around a hyperlink when you click it in Internet Explorer may seem like a nuisance, but they really do serve a purpose. Focus lines are an Accessibility feature that helps users see whether they've clicked the desired hyperlink or which hyperlink they previously clicked if they click the browser's Back button. If for your purposes the focus lines are unwanted, you can

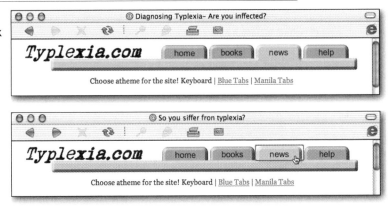

get rid of them with a little JavaScript magic. Locate the hyperlink in Dreamweaver and then use the Tag inspector to add an `onClick` event with a value of `if(this.blur)` `this.blur();`. The resulting code would look something like this: `<a href=` `"home.html" onClick="if(this.blur)this.blur();">Link</a>` Now preview the page in Internet Explorer. Before you click the link, you must chant "Focus Pocus" while spinning around three times or it won't work.

   LEARNING TO ACCESSORIZE

You don't need to be a fashion diva to accessorize your browser with trendy, hip, cool features. Adding accessories to your browser will make surfing easier and testing websites much quicker and cleaner. You'll be able to make a selection, right-click (Ctrl+click), and select View Partial Source, which will show you the source code of only your selection. No more scrolling through endless lines of code to find the single line you need. That's just one of many features you can add to your browser. No matter how I describe the features, you can't get a clear picture of their usefulness without trying them first. You can find

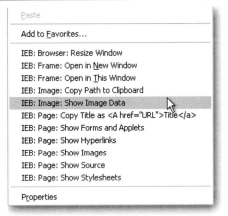

the accessories at two locations I know, depending on your flavor of Internet Explorer. Internet Explorer 5.x: `http://www.microsoft.com/windows/ie/previous/` `webaccess/default.asp`. Internet Explorer 6.x: `http://www.paessler.com/` `products/ieb/`.

  BROWSER EMULATORS & ARCHIVES

You too can become a browser-testing fanatic. For all your development testing needs, a collection of varying browser versions have been archived at http://browsers.evolt.org/. Do you ever wonder what your web page looks like on a version 2.0 browser? Don't bother installing an old browser just to satisfy your curiosity. Instead, head on over to a site that specializes in browser emulation, such as http://www.dejavu.org/. If a client is

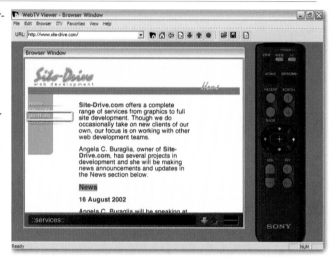

concerned with Web TV, you needn't worry about getting it just for him. There's the Web TV Viewer available for testing your websites:http://developer.msntv.com/Tools/WebTVVwr.asp.

   CAN YOU SPARE ME THE CACHE?

For the most part, allowing a browser to cache a page is a good thing. Instead of loading every page element each time the user visits, the browser checks the user's computer for a locally stored version. When providing up-to-date informa-

tion is critical, you don't want the user viewing an old page. Click the Meta object in the Head category of the Insert bar. Select http-equiv from the Attributes drop-down list, type **pragma** in the Value field, type **no-cache** in the Content field, and then click OK. Most browsers obey `<meta>` tags, but to be extra sure you could use some server-side techniques as discussed in Chapter 8, "*Greased Lightning:* Application Building Tips."

  ONLY TEMPORARY

When you are viewing a page in the browser using Dreamweaver's Preview in Browser feature, depending on your Preferences, either the real page or a temporary one is displayed. Some folks just don't like temporary files, even though they're great for restoring to a previous version if you screw up or crash. With Dreamweaver MX you're no longer confined to using temporary files for browser preview. Deselect the checkbox labeled Preview Using Temporary File in Preferences. The setting also affects Server Debugging used with ColdFusion, which lets you use Dreamweaver's interface as a browser.

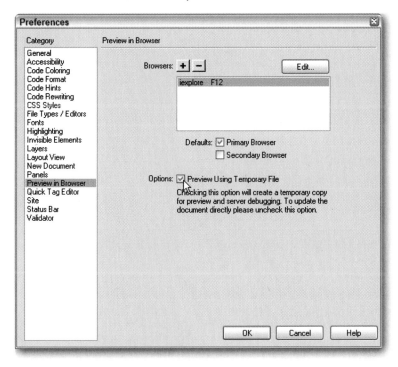

  USER-DEFINED STYLES

As modern browsers make it easier for people to use their own custom style sheet on any given site, it is becoming increasingly important that you design your pages to good (X)HTML standards. You too can take advantage of using your own style sheets while browsing the web or testing your own websites. In Mozilla, there is even a View > Use Style submenu. In Internet Explorer, select Tools > Internet Options and then click the Accessibility button. In the dialog that appears, you can browse to a specific CSS file on your hard drive or point to an absolute URL. Knowing that this is possible for users means that you will be aware of how you

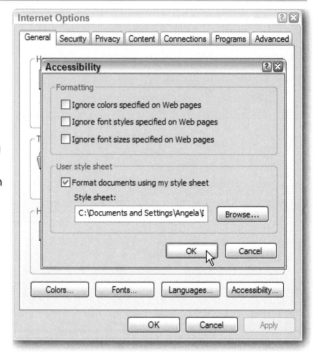

code so that your site will look its best no matter which style sheet is used—yours or theirs. If you're handy with CSS, you can hide elements so that they are not a distraction to you as you preview in the browser. By modifying your user-defined CSS file while leaving the real one in place, you can do testing live on the site without disrupting the look until you're ready to replace the current file. Have fun with this one; you'll find it is a great way to learn all about CSS.

    MULTIPLE PREVIEWS

There have been many times
that I've needed to work with
multiple files and preview
them in the browser. So I
open them all up and then
one by one I press F12 to view
them. This was a major "Duh!"
moment when I realized that
I can preview them all in
one shot. In the Site Panel,
Ctrl+click each file you need
to preview or click once and
then Shift+click a few files
away to get all files between
the first and second click.
Use the Preview in Browser
keyboard shortcut F12
(primary browser) or
Shift+F12 (secondary
browser) or right-click
(Ctrl+click) the selection in
the Site panel and choose
your browser from the

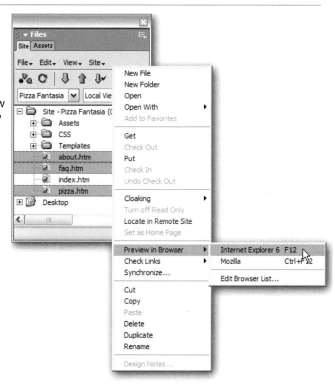

Preview in Browser submenu. All the pages will open in the same window so that you can
use your browser's Back button to navigate between pages.

Speed of
Light Layouts

*Dreamweaver users know "layers"
as* `<div>` *tags that use an absolute
position defined within inline styles.
Whether you call them layers or by any other*

Speed of Light Layouts

advanced layout tips

*name, it doesn't matter to me. (Hey, whatever
makes you happy. I mean, you can call them
shnicklegroobers for all I care, really.) But
sooner or later you're going to need layers
for a project and you're going to want to
know all the coolest tips for using them in
Dreamweaver. You may even get so inspired
that you'll try to design your very first site
without tables—unless you need to display
tabular data, of course.*

*Frames have caused many developers I
know to lose a few hairs and gain a few gray
ones. Don't let this happen to you. Learn from
our experiences and see how easy developing
a frame-based site can be. Even if you don't
like frames, you'll at the very least find some
great entertainment value in these tips.*

*Now that you know what is in this chapter,
why are you still reading this introduction? Go
on, turn the page and indulge yourself in the
wealth of knowledge that awaits you. <sigh>
You're still reading this…</sigh> Fine, I'll just
end this introduction right now so that you
can stop wasting time and get on with
the chapter.*

CHANGING LAYER STACKING ORDER

A layer's stacking order is controlled by the z-index. The higher the z-index, the closer to the front the layer appears in the browser. When you are working with multiple layers and need to change the z-index property, you will find that using the Property inspector can be a bit monotonous and tedious. The Layers panel (choose Window > Others > Layers or press F2) makes changing the z-index much easier. Click and drag the layer name within the Layers panel to where you want the layer to appear and automatically each layer's z-index property will be adjusted to the new order. If you want to change a single layer's z-index without affecting the other layers, click the number in the Z column and type the new z-index value. When you're done, either press Enter (Return) or click elsewhere in the workspace.

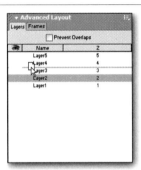

LAYERS LIKE YOU LIKE 'EM

Adding a layer is simple when you use the Insert > Layer command or the Draw Layer object found in the Common category of the Insert bar. After inserting a layer, chances are that you'll need to make changes to its styles using the Property inspector. What you may not know is that you can save yourself the time and trouble of doing the same changes with each layer by setting your Layer preferences. Select Edit > Preferences (Dreamweaver > Preferences on Mac OS X) or Ctrl+U (Command+U) and then choose the Layers category listed on the left. There you'll find various settings that will be used when you insert a layer. The Width and Height fields will affect only layers that you insert with the Insert > Layer command. Change this preference as often as you like to help speed up your layer production.

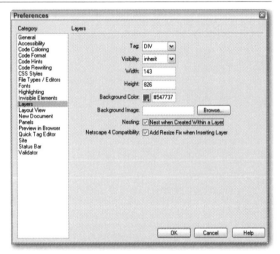

98   CHAPTER 5 • Advanced Layout Tips

DRAWING MULTIPLE CONSECUTIVE LAYERS

Often when I am working with layers, I need to draw several at once. I used to click the Draw Layer button in the Common category of the Insert bar (way back when it was called the *Objects panel*), draw my layer, and then repeat. Click button, draw layer. Click button, draw layer. That got old real quick. I soon discovered that there is indeed a better way to do this. All you need to do is hold the Ctrl (Command) key while clicking and dragging out your layer, and when you are finished, you'll still have the crosshairs that indicate you can draw another one.

MOVIN' AND GROOVIN' AND LAYIN' TO THE BEAT NOW

We were movin' and groovin' and jamming to the beat, just when it hit me and I heard somebody shout, "Drag that layer by its shield now. Drag that layer where you want!" Don't you sing while you work? Assuming that you know the tune "Play That Funky Music" by Wild Cherry, you'll never be able to drag a layer by its shield again without thinking of

this tip. When you have a layer selected, its corresponding anchor point (that little yellow shield-looking thingy) also is highlighted. If you click and drag the layer by its anchor point the corresponding code is moved right along with it, effectively changing the order of your code and shields. If you don't see what I'm talking about, make sure that View > Visual Aids > Invisible Elements is enabled. If you've previously disabled them, turn on Invisible Elements for Anchor Points for Layers in Preferences.

NOW YOU SEE IT, NOW YOU DON'T

You needn't be a DHTML wizard to show and hide layers. Dreamweaver makes it easy with the Show-Hide Layers behavior. Draw a layer where you want it to appear. Now select the link, be it text or an image that

will trigger the event, and then select the Show-Hide Layers behavior from the Add (+) button's drop-down list on the Behaviors panel. Each layer is listed by its ID in the Named Layers field. Select each layer that you want to show or hide with this event and then click the Show or Hide button. The Default button will reset the layer so that its current state is unchanged by this event. Just think of all the cool menus you can create using this behavior.

THE CLIENT WHO MUST HAVE HOVER

Clients…some of them are just too picky.
We can explain site design issues to them
until the cows come home, but they don't
always "get it." Here's a kludge to
appease those clients who just don't
understand why their links can change
color in Internet Explorer but not in
Netscape 4.x. Add a link to a layer, and
then make an exact duplicate of the layer
but change the color of the link with CSS.
Now apply the Show-Hide Layers behavior to the link `onMouseOver` to create
the illusion of the hover psuedoclass in

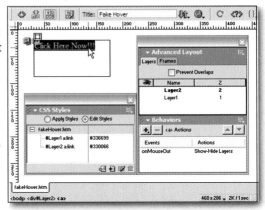

Netscape 4.x. On the link that is displayed onMouseover, you'll want to apply the Show/Hide
Layers behavior again. This time you'll need to hide the layer onMouseOut and show the
original layer again. This certainly adds more code to the page, which you should take under
consideration or you'll end up with pages that take too long to load. Although it may be
overkill to take this route, you'll save your sanity, your client will be happy, and you can
move on to other things.

   PUT THOSE LAYERS IN THEIR PLACE

Check out a Dreamweaver-generated page designed with
Layers in Netscape 4.x and then change the size of your
browser window. Notice that the page reloads?
Dreamweaver adds what is known as the Netscape Resize
Fix script to the page whenever a layer is inserted or drawn.
Without this script, layers would not be in their proper
place when users resize their browsers, which can get
pretty messy. Dreamweaver doesn't add the script if
you've inserted a `<div>` that has its positioning declared
in the `<head>` of your page or in an external CSS file;
it only knows to add it if the CSS is inline. You'll find the

Add/Remove Netscape Resize Fix in the Commands menu, which will ask if you'd like to add
the script if it is not already on the page, otherwise it will ask you if you'd like to remove the
script. If you decide to put the script in an external JavaScript file, you may want to visit the
Layers category of Edit > Preferences (Dreamweaver > Preferences on Mac OS X) to disable
the automatic insertion of the code each time a Layer is inserted by Dreamweaver.

SUPERSIZING LAYERS

Getting the size of a layer just right by using its resize handles takes a little hand-eye coordination—something I know I lack after a long day. What I prefer is to use keyboard shortcuts to size the layers exactly the way I need them. With a layer already selected, I use Ctrl+any arrow key (Option+any arrow key) to size the layer pixel by pixel. If I want to change the size by 10 pixels or more, I use Ctrl+Shift+ any arrow key (Option+Shift+any arrow key) to change the layer's size in 10-pixel increments. You may be thinking that you could just use the Property inspector to change the appropriate values, but I find that this method is much faster when you're not sure of the values and must see the changes to know that you've got it right. If you've enabled View > Grid > Snap to Grid the shortcuts mentioned here will work together with that feature providing similar results and can speed things up for you even more.

   TAKING PREVENTATIVE MEASURES

If you decide to use the Property inspector to change a layer's values of Width, Height, Left, or Top, be sure to include a pixel(px) or percentage(%) measurement immediately following the integer. Dreamweaver doesn't require that you enter a unit of measurement, but modern browsers that support DTDs (doctypes) will not respond well if the unit of measurement is missing. So if you're experiencing placement issues in a browser, one of the first things to check is that the unit of measurement for the property was included.

   PIXEL-PERFECT POSITIONING

Putting a layer in its place can be a bit tedious when you need pixel-perfect positioning. It gets easier when you remember that you can move a selected layer by using your arrow keys, and you can move it in 10-pixel increments by pressing Shift+any arrow key.

  NO TRESPASSING

You can keep new layers from overlapping existing layers without doing any math to calculate positioning. Even if it is simple addition and subtraction, who wants to do math? Dreamweaver has a special command you can enable and disable at will that prevents layers you insert with the Draw Layer object from overlapping. You'll see a black circle with a

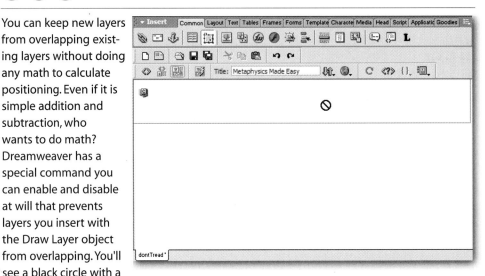

line through it if you try to add a layer where a layer already exists. If you drag an existing layer, Dreamweaver won't let you trespass on other layers. The Prevent Layer Overlaps command is rather hidden in the Modify > Arrange submenu. A more convenient location is at the top of the Layers panel, where you'll find a Prevent Overlaps checkbox.

   SOMETIMES THE OBVIOUS ESCAPES US

If you're like me, sometimes the obvious escapes you—pun very much intended, as you'll soon see. After you click that Draw Layer icon, you're stuck with the cross-hairs until you draw a layer. However, if you press the Esc key, you'll be freed from that cursor and won't have to draw a layer after all. A single click in the document without dragging also will free you of the cursor. I'd rather use the Esc key than go through the process of adding something unwanted only to undo it. In fact, using the Esc key has the same cancellation effect for most situations in Dreamweaver in which you might change your mind.

NESTING URGES

Feeling the urge to nest some layers? As long as you don't allow trespassers (see the earlier tip, "No Trespassing"), you can use a few techniques to make the process painless. Hold down the Alt (Option) key while clicking and dragging over another layer for an easy approach to nesting layers. If you will be doing a lot of nesting, there is a Preference setting you should know about. Select Edit > Preferences (Dreamweaver > Preferences on Mac OS X) or Ctrl+U (Command+U) and then choose the Layers category listed on the left. Notice the checkbox labeled: Nest When

Created Within a Layer? If that checkbox is marked, whenever you start to draw a layer with the Draw Layer object while your cursor is over another layer—even without holding the Alt (Option) key—the new layer will end up nested inside the existing layer. Another approach to nesting layers is to click inside a layer, and then use the Insert > Layer object. There you have it: three ways to nest a layer using Dreamweaver. Not enough you say? You want another method? Okay, how about Ctrl+click-n-drag (Command+click-n-drag) the name of an existing layer in the panel and release the mouse key when the layer is over what will become the parent layer. You'll know you've got it right when you see the Layers panel listing layers in a tree-menu type of format.

   CHANGE LAYER CONTENTS

There is no need to make the user wait for an entire new page to load when all you want to change is a single layer's contents. Don't let the name fool you; the Set Text of Layer behavior does more than change text in a layer. You'll need at least one layer on the page

before you can click the Behaviors panel's Add (+) button and select Set Text > Set Text of Layer. In the dialog that appears, you'll notice it says New HTML. Try using any HTML you want—good old copy and paste comes in handy in situations like this. As long as the browser understands it, that code will be represented in the layer. Be sure that the event listed in the Behaviors panel is set the way you want it and then go ahead and preview the page.

You might be wondering, "Why not use Show/Hide Layers and use as many layers as needed?" One benefit is that the layer will always have the same ID and other attributes. This means that the look of the layer can remain consistent without repeating the same code.

BUSINESS AS USUAL

Just because you prefer to not use inline styles—because you've learned the benefits of externalizing your CSS—when creating layers, doesn't mean that you can't take advantage of the fields in the Property inspector for layers. When you want to edit the ID Selector in an external CSS file, you don't have to edit the CSS file manually or by using the CSS Style Definition dialog. Dreamweaver doesn't care whether your CSS is inline or external; it is just business as usual. You can modify the values in the Property inspector or drag and adjust the layer itself within the document, and Dreamweaver updates the external CSS file.

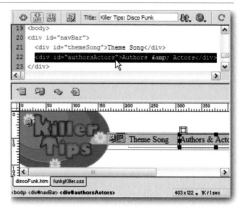

Just in case you're a little confused, a layer in Dreamweaver might have an opening tag that looks something like this: `<div id=" contentLayer" style="position:absolute; left:395px; top:55px; width:62px; height:45px; z-index:2">`. You can remove all the values of the style attribute and put them into an external stylesheet using an ID selector. (See "Can I See Some Identification, Please?" in Chapter 2 for more about ID selectors.) If you're working in this fashion, don't forget to upload the external CSS file to see the changes online.

WHY SO BLUE?

Ever wonder why the icons representing

the Frame objects found on the Insert bar look the way they do? Every icon has one area shown in a light blue color. Sure, it's stylish—but it's also purposeful. The blue area represents where the current page is placed when a Frame object is applied. So the first icon, called Left Frame, places your existing content on the right and the second icon, called Right Frame, puts the current page on the left. I find the object names somewhat misleading (yeah, like BMW's are somewhat expensive) so I just go by the icon to pick the style I want.

FRAMESETS-A-POLOOZA

If you've used any of the Frames objects in previous versions, you know that Dreamweaver incorporates the current page into the created frameset. But what if you are starting from scratch, know you want a particular style of frameset, but you don't have a page to start with? Before Dreamweaver MX, you had to open a blank page and apply a Frames object; now you can skip that intermediate step and open a

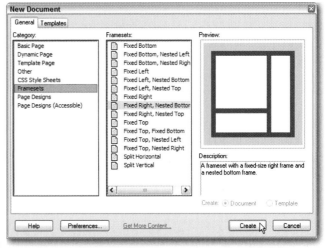

new frameset page and be ready to go. Dreamweaver's New Document dialog includes a Framesets category with all the same formats available as Frames objects. Just choose one and Dreamweaver creates all the pages you need, leaving your current page alone.

   QUICK DRAW FRAMESETS

The Frames objects are pretty swift—in fact, they're so nifty that many folks don't realize that you can drag out a frameset manually. To create a frameset by dragging, choose View > Visual Aids > Frame Borders (or select the same menu option from the View Options button on the Document toolbar). Then, press Alt (Option) and drag out one of the borders. You even can instantly create a frameset with four frames by

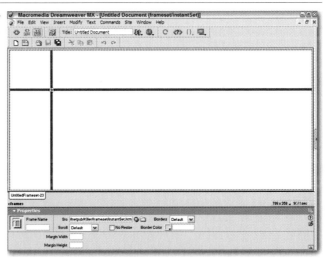

dragging in the frame border corner—try that, Frame objects!

SPLITS ARE ALL RELATIVE

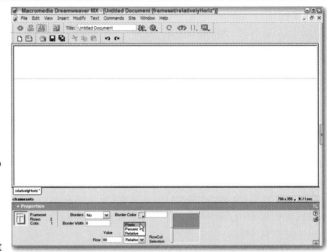

Almost all the standard framesets created by the Frames objects or the New Documents dialog involve one or more frames with a set pixel width or height. Put in a Fixed Left frameset, for example, and the left frame has a width of 80 pixels. (For whatever reason, 80 seems to be one of the Dreamweaver engineers' favorite numbers—all the frames with set values are set to 80 pixels.) The two exceptions to the set pattern are the Split Horizontal and Split Vertical framesets. Apply either of these frame objects and your page is—well, split—into two sections, both using the relative measurement. This brings me to the "Gotcha!"—resize either of these split framesets and, instead of one or both frames switching to a fixed pixel width, they both remain relative values. Depending on the size of your frames, this could mean that some of your content might not be seen on smaller browser windows. (By the way, you can get into the same spot of trouble by choosing any of the Split Frame options under Modify > Frameset.) The solution here is to select the frameset and, from the Property inspector, change one of the frames from Relative to Pixels units.

A FRAMESET BY ANY OTHER NAMESET

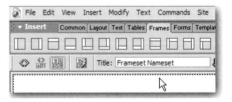

How many times have you been surfing the web and come across a frame-based page where the browser window displays "Untitled Documents"? How many times has that been one of your sites? Incorrectly titling a frameset is a fairly common mistake—many times, designers give one of the frames the desired title instead of the frameset, which is where is needs to be. Before entering the title in Dreamweaver's Document toolbar, make sure that you've selected the frameset border. When you go back to entering content in one of the frames, the title will disappear—but that's to be expected. Select the frameset border again and the title will reappear in Dreamweaver and be there when the pages are uploaded to the web.

GETTING IN TOUCH WITH YOUR INNER FRAMESET

Nested framesets are often the best choice for a complex layout—but they can be difficult to modify. The key to making changes to a nested frameset is choosing the right one. You'll find the key at the bottom of the window in the area called the Tag Selector. Click any frameset border to identify which frameset you're using. If you see only one frameset tag in the Tag Selector, you've selected the outermost frameset. Select another border, and when you see two such tags—

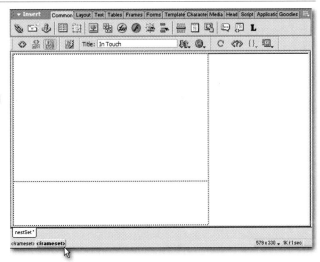

that is, `<frameset> <frameset>`—choose the rightmost one to select the inner frameset. With an extremely complex layout—say, three or more nested framesets—you may have to select a few different borders to identify the desired frameset.

   ### KEEPING FRAMES IN THEIR PLACE

Because framesets are comprised of separate pages, it's entirely possible for a user to browse directly to a page—from a search engine, for example—and have no idea it's supposed to be part of a frameset. One way to handle this problem is to put this code in the `<head>` of every file in the frameset:

```
<script language="JavaScript">
if (top == self) self.location.href = "FramesetFileName";
</script>
```

In this code, *FramesetFileName* is the name of the frameset the file is part of. This code looks to see whether the page is within a frameset and if not, puts it in its intended place. Notice that this code is triggered only if the page is not in a frameset; it doesn't matter whether it is in the proper frameset. For a more complete solution, see Hal Pawluk's FrameJammer and FrameStuffer extensions on the Dreamweaver Exchange (accessible by choosing Help > Dreamweaver Exchange).

HELP I'VE BEEN FRAMED, AGAIN!

Here's a tip to handle the opposite problem posed in the previous tip. How do you keep your pages from being frame-napped and placed in someone else's frameset against their (and your) will? Here's the JavaScript to place in pages you want to keep frameless:

```
<script language="JavaScript">
if (self.parent.frames.length!=0){
        self.parent.location.replace(document.location.href)
}
</script>
```

If you want to keep your hand-coding to a minimum, another solution is to add Andrew Wooldridge's Bust Frames or Rabi Sunder Raj's Frame Buster extension (available from the Dreamweaver Exchange) to your page. Both approaches work the same way: they look to see whether any frames are in use and bust out of them if they're found.

   PLAYING THE FRAME NAME GAME

Everyone who has worked with frames has had this experience. You start work on your frameset and get far enough along that you're ready to preview the page, so you press F12, Preview in Browser. Dreamweaver requires that all elements—each of the pages and the

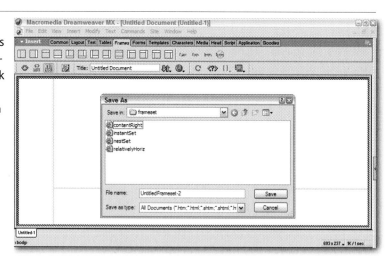

frameset(s)—be saved before previewing, so the Save File dialog pops up. But how do you name a file if you don't know which file you're naming? The preset names (`Untitled-7.htm`, `Untitled-8.htm`, etc.) are not much help. Luckily, Dreamweaver gives you a couple of clues, if you know where to look. Framesets are always saved first and a special generic name is used: `UntitledFrameset-X`, where X represents an incrementing number. The biggest clue, however, is visual: Dreamweaver identifies what frame it is asking you to save by placing a dotted, black border around the frame in the Document window. If it is a frameset (nested or otherwise), more than one frame is enclosed.

HELP, I'VE BEEN FRAMED

In some ways Dreamweaver's
Frames objects are too easy
to apply. You may start out
with a frame design and
realize that you need to alter
the layout to go with one less
frame or no frames at all. So
how do you get rid of a frame
already in place? One way is
to remove the border that
creates the frame. No, you
don't delete the border; you
drag the border to the edge
of the Document window,
and that removes the frame
from the frameset. Of course,
if you have content in the
page removed from the
frameset and you've already
saved the document, the
content is still available;
just open the file.

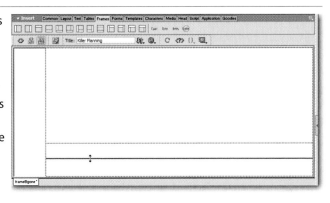

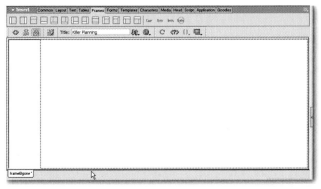

   TARGETTING MULTIPLE FRAMES

The vast majority of the time, a link in a
frameset is intended to load a page in a
single frame. Sometimes, though, a single
link is needed to update multiple frames.
There are two ways to approach this
problem. The first method is to link to

another frameset that corresponds to the targeted pages; this works well when the pages
that are changing are associated. The only real negative is that it adds another layer of
complexity to managing the site. The other method is to use a standard link in addition
to a Dreamweaver Go To URL behavior—the link opens one page in a targeted frame and
the behavior opens another page in a different frame. The downside to the second
approach is that it will take two clicks of the browser's Back button for the user to return
to the previous location.

OODLES OF UNDO-ODLES

If you know anything about frames, you know that each frameset is made up of multiple files—but here's something you may not realize: each of the frames has an independent undo memory or stack. This means that you can make a change in one of your frames, switch to another, and use Undo (Ctrl+Z or Command+Z) and the change in the other frame will not be undone. You must select the frame containing the change you want reversed. A real graphic way to see this is to open the History panel (Windows > Others > History) and then click into each and every one of your frames—the History panel will display different steps for every one. Even the frameset itself, an independent HTML file, has its own undo stack.

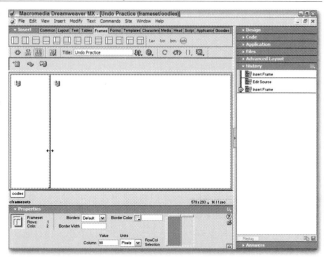

Bonus tip: To undo the application of a frameset, after choosing one of the Frame objects, select Undo twice. The first Undo will display the page split vertically into two frames, and the second brings it back to a frameset-less state.

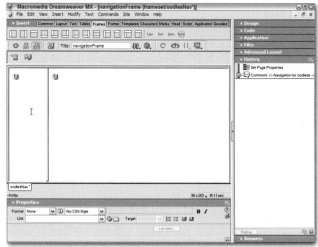

CREATING ACCESSIBLE FRAMES

The Section 508 Accessibility guidelines require that frames be titled with understandable names that assist navigation. The key word here is *titled*. It is not enough for your frames to have appropriate names, like `navigation` or `content`; additionally, each `<frame>` also must have a `title` attribute with similar values. (The name and title attributes

don't have to be the same, although that's often the easiest course.) The `title` attribute can, of course, be added by hand or by selecting the `<frame>` tag in Code view and entering the `title` value in the Tag inspector. The other technique for making sure your frameset is compliant with Section 508 is to enable the Frames option in the Accessibility category of Preferences. Once enabled, the Frame Tag Accessibility Attributes dialog appears whenever a frameset is created. To title the frames, choose the frame name from the drop-down list and enter the desired title in the bottom field; be sure to cycle through all the frame names. The Frame Tag Accessibility Attributes dialog (say that five times fast!) does not appear, however, if you create the frameset by dragging out a frame border.

  ## DÉJÀ VU FRAMES

Looking to play a trick on fellow web designers? Throw a little recursion their way. To make a recursive frame, first set a link on a frameset to the frameset itself. Next, set the target of that link to `_self`. When selected, the page with the recursive link will be replaced by the entire frameset—which is already within the frameset. Select the link again and you've got a frameset within a frameset within a frameset. You can

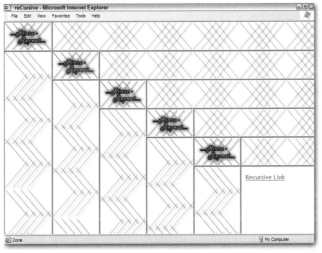

recursively display a frameset with about three or four iterations before they "blow up real good" as the boys on SCTV used to say. Of course, if you want to avoid recursive framesets, set that target to `_top`—but then you'd just be a spoil sport.

Rev Your Engines

Template Library

Are you the kind of web designer who lovingly crafts each bit of code that goes into the page? Someone who, if you could, would sculpt the angle brackets

Rev Your Engines

templates, library, and production tips

that surround each HTML tag? If that description fits you like a wet t-shirt, then skip right over this chapter. This chapter is for working folks, designers who need to get the job done—get it done right, of course—the most efficient way possible. Because the web designer's job is an ongoing one, implementing the design and updating the site must be as easy and thorough as possible. If that sounds like Dreamweaver templates and library items to you, you're in the right place. You want to know how much of a geek I am? When Macromedia added repeating and optional regions as well as editable attributes in Dreamweaver MX, I partied for three days—and believe me, Dreamweaver geeks know how to party.

Throughout this chapter, you'll find tips detailing how best to use these advanced features and more (we threw in some general production tips for good measure). By this chapter's end, I expect to see you whipping out templates with one hand, inserting library items with the other while dancing an Irish jig. Or maybe a Texas two-step…anything but that Macarena dance; I'm flexible…to a point.

EASYMAKE TEMPLATES

If you're looking to create a template, Dreamweaver MX has paved a few new routes for you to try. Now, you can use the New Document dialog and choose the Basic Page category from the first column and HTML Template from the second. If you're working dynamically, select the Template Page category and choose the desired server model/language from the second column. Either of these actions will create a blank template with only two editable regions in place, one for the document title and a generic one for other head elements.

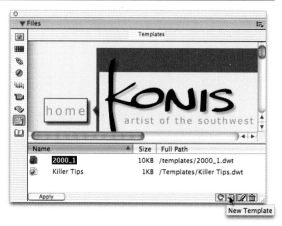

Prefer a more immediate approach? Select the New Template button from the Templates category of the Assets panel. You also can choose New Template from the Assets panel Options menu.

Would you rather convert an existing page to a template than start from scratch? You're familiar with the old Save As Template command in the File menu, right? In addition to that tried-and-true technique, Dreamweaver MX adds a new wrinkle or two. From the Templates category of the Insert bar, choose Make Template to convert the current standard document to template format. Inserting any of the other template objects causes Dreamweaver automatically to turn the document into a template. However, you won't see the familiar `<<Template>>` designation in the title bar until you save the file.

   ### EDIBLE PEARS VERSUS EDITABLE PAIRS

When you're marking an area of your document as an editable region, you need to make sure that you're working with complete tag pairs. You either need to select content within a tag pair, like `<p> . . . </p>`, or select the tag pair itself. If you don't, Dreamweaver expands the selection until its overlapping tags are enclosed before applying the editable region—and there's no warning that your selection isn't proper. For example, let's say you want to make a column in a table editable. You'd think you'd be able to choose the column and then select Editable Region from the Insert bar Templates category, right? Wrong. The column designation has no equivalent in HTML tags and so Dreamweaver will mark as editable all the rows containing cells within the selected column. The right, albeit tedious, way to make a column editable is to separately mark each cell (`<td> . . . </td>`) in the column as an editable region.

KEEPING IT STYLISH

Part of the reason templates have proved so popular is that they allow the designer to specify a consistent look-and-feel while allowing the content to vary. If you're not careful how you define your editable regions in templates, however, you could lose the control over style. When selecting the content for an editable region, be careful not to include any formatting elements that could be altered. For example, if you

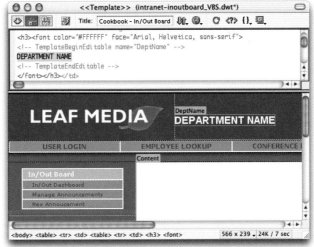

want to make sure that your heading remains a `<h3>` style, select only the text within the tag, not the tag itself. If you include the `<h3>`...`</h3>` tag pair, it could easily be changed to another heading style in the document derived from the template. I frequently stay in the split-view mode to see both code and the design elements and ensure that I have selected only what I want to remain editable. When using CSS, the style sheet declarations (whether you are working with external or internal styles) should remain in the locked part of the template.

A REGION BY ANY OTHER NAME WOULD SMELL AS SWEET

Does it matter what you name your template regions? Template region names are not as sensitive as other object names, like those for layers or images, but there are limits. Certain special characters are not allowed: the ampersand

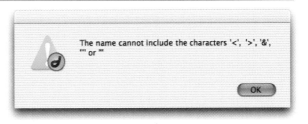

(&), double quote ("), single quote a.k.a. apostrophe ('), and the left and right angle brackets (< and >). Moreover, each region's name must be unique among other template regions in the same template. In other words, it's possible to have a layer and an editable region both named `content`. Is that a good idea? Probably not, but that's never stopped anyone before, so why should you be different?

HEADS UP!

Here's a feature new to Dreamweaver MX that may have slipped in under your radar. You may have previously noticed that Dreamweaver enclosed the `<title>` tag in its own editable region called `doctitle`. Now, whenever you create a template, in addition to this, Dreamweaver now adds a second editable region to the `<head>` area, called, appropriately enough, `head`. You probably won't have much use for the `head` editable region during the template creation phase, but it is truly invaluable when working with documents created from a template. Any `<meta>` tags needed for a document derived from a template are inserted in the `head` region. Likewise, any `<script>` tags (and their content) necessary for Dreamweaver behaviors are placed there.

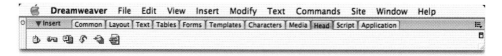

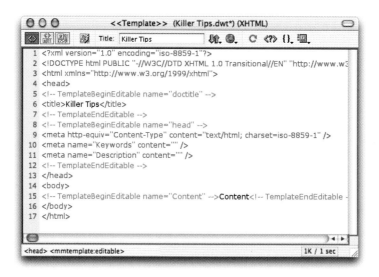

DA LINK'S DA TING

What's the number one problem folks have with templates? Links. Web designers used to coding links by hand are frequently tripped up when working with templates. Here's why: When a document is derived from the template, Dreamweaver automatically adjusts the links so that they point to the proper file. But for Dreamweaver to handle this operation correctly, the links must point to the right file from the template itself (which is stored in the Templates folder, in the site root). A common mistake is to try to create a link to a file as though the template were the derived document.

Here's an example. Let's say famed designer Joe Schmoe is working with a Dreamweaver template and creates a link to a widgets.htm page in the products folder. Joe thinks, "I know the pages I'm going to create from this template will all be located in the root folder, and the products folder is also in the root, so I'll just write in the link like this, products/widgets.htm." I'm afraid Mr. Schmoe has made a *faux pas*. The correct link in the template would be ../products/widgets.htm—which Dreamweaver would convert to products/widgets.htm in a document derived from the template.

The best way to ensure that you are assigning the correct links in a template is to always use the Browse for File or Point to File options found on the Property inspector next to the Link field. If you're linking to a file that doesn't exist yet, use Browse for File to link to another file in the same folder and change the file's name by hand.

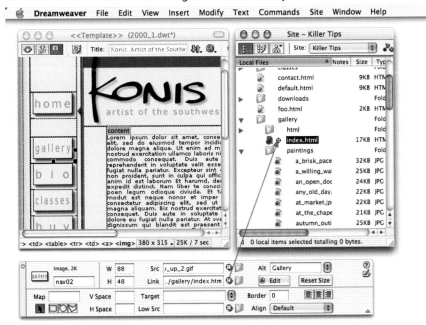

  STAY TUNED FOR A SPECIAL UPDATE

With both library items and templates, when you save the document, you are asked whether you want to update pages. Maybe you decided not to update because you realized you made a mistake, or you have some other good reason. Perhaps you agreed to update files, but in the summary that follows an update you notice a few files were not updated. Most likely, you'll use this if you decided to use an external editor to make changes to the template or library file. In any case, if ever you need them, the Update Current Page and Update Pages commands are there in the Modify menu under the Library and Templates submenus. You'll also find Update Current Page in the context menu and in the Options menu of the Templates and Library categories of the Assets panel, but instead of Update Pages, you'll see Update Site (same thing, different name). Naturally these commands work only if a template or library item is already in use with a document. When using the Update Pages or Update Site command, you'll be shown the Update

Pages dialog. Whether Library or Templates is checked depends on how you arrived at the dialog, but you can definitely choose both and make your updates lickity split.

   QUICK EDITABLE REGIONS

When you are building a template from scratch, you can quickly add editable regions without having to select any existing content. Just position the cursor where you'd like the editable region to appear and choose Insert > Template Objects > Editable Region. If you're feeling dexterous, choose Ctrl+Alt+V (Command+Option+V). Want to point and click? Select the Editable Region object from the Insert bar, Templates category. All these methods will give you a chance to name the region and then put that name, as text, in the editable region. If I'm passing the template on to someone else, I try to replace the text—which also appears in the identifying tab —with something more meaningful, like "Bio info on author goes here." One other note on working with Dreamweaver-inserted editable regions: If you decide to remove the region, the included text stays behind and becomes part of your locked template, which means that you'll have to delete that text manually.

  ## CHANGING YOUR MIND ABOUT TEMPLATE REGIONS

The previous tip ended with a brief warning about removing the
editable region markup. While I'm in the general vicinity, let me fill
you in on some other tips to keep in mind when deleting template
markup. First off, do you know how to convert an editable region
back to a locked area? Place your cursor within the editable region
and choose Modify > Templates > Remove Template Markup; this
option also is available from the context menu. The same process is
used to get rid of an optional or a repeating
region. It's also handy to note when removing an
optional region that the region's corresponding
TemplateParam statement is not removed. You'll
have to hunt those little buggers down and axe
'em yourself.

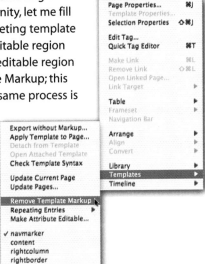

Finally, how do you get rid of all the template
markup from a page? Although you could go
through and select each template region
individually, and then choose the Remove
Template Markup command, a far faster method is to create a document from the template
and then choose Modify > Templates > Detach from Template.

   ## ZAP THAT TEMPLATE? THINK TWICE (OR EVEN THRICE!)

When it comes time to do a little site maintenance, be extra careful about removing
templates. They're extremely easy to delete and have profound consequences. Just select
one and choose the Delete icon in the Templates category of the Assets panel and, *poof!*
the file is gone, along with any way of updating documents derived from that template.
Dreamweaver doesn't utter a word of protest—not a peep!—alerting you to the fact that a
number of files will be orphaned. One way to see which files are derived from a template is
to make a minor update—like adding a space at the end of the template file—and then
saving the template. If Dreamweaver doesn't find any pages derived from that template in
the current site, the Update Pages dialog is not displayed and you'll know it's safe to delete
the template.

  THE TWIN TABS

When you have a template filled with editable regions of varying types, it can be tough to tell one type of region from another in a quick glance. Setting distinctive colors in the Highlighting category of Edit > Preferences (Dreamweaver > Preferences on Mac OS X) can make distinguishing among regions much easier. If the tabs just drive you crazy and are getting in the way of your design, you can disable them here in the same Preferences category by unchecking the box in the

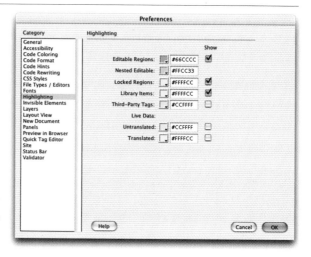

Show column. Alternatively, you can toggle them on and off by choosing View > Visual Aids > Invisible Elements.

   EDITABLE ATTRIBUTES BLAST-OFF

Of all the new template enhancements introduced in Dreamweaver MX, I'm particularly fond of editable attributes. With this feature (accessible by choosing Modify > Templates > Make Attribute Editable), you can unlock only the essential aspects of an object, like a table row's background color, while keeping everything else (the alignment, the class, and so on) safe and secure. As with most new features, there is a bit of a learning curve in figuring out

how to best work with editable attributes. Here's a tip that will help you skip a couple of steps in the set-up process. Whenever possible, make sure that your tag already includes the attribute you plan to make editable. Although the Editable Tag Attributes dialog allows you to add any attribute you want, if the attribute is already in the tag—whether or not it has a value—you can simply pick it from a drop-down list. Otherwise, you have to choose Add and fill in the attribute name.

120　CHAPTER 6 • Templates, Library, and Production Tips

EDITABLE ATTRIBUTES, TWO FOR TWO

Here are a couple more pointers worth sharing that can help you work with editable attributes. Numerous attributes—like width or height—require a numeric value, or what appears to be a numeric value. Because the attributes could actually be a percent or pixel designation, such as 75%, the value is really text. Therefore, when you are setting up your editable attributes in a template, specify the type as Text rather than Number. If you choose Number and try to enter a percentage or pixel value, Dreamweaver will bark at you when you save the template.

Ready for another tidbit? After you establish an editable attribute, you can apply it to as many tags as you like. This capability is quite handy when you want various elements on the page to share a characteristic. You could, for example, change the background image of a table cell on multiple tables. To apply the attribute in various tags, just copy and paste the attribute that includes the template variable.

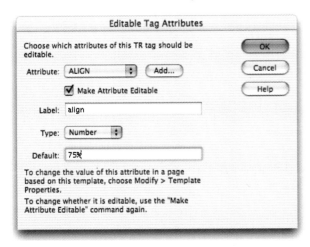

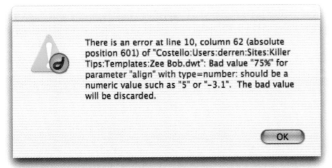

  THE DARK SIDE OF EDITABLE ATTRIBUTES

Ok, so I've waxed poetic about editable attributes for the last couple of tips. Does sliced bread still wear the crown as the coolest thing? Unfortunately, yes. You also should note that, in my view, editable attributes have a significant flaw: after you make an attribute editable, it no longer is rendered in Design view when editing the template. For example, let's say you make the background color of a table cell editable—you even choose a reasonable default color. When editing the template in Code view, the attribute will look like this:

```
bgcolor="@@(tdcolor)@@"
```

Dreamweaver doesn't properly interpret the variable name as the `bgcolor` value (unlike with template instances), so it acts as though it isn't there. This is particularly noticeable when your design actually includes the attribute. Unfortunately, there's really not a work-around for this problem. You can, however, kvetch about it and gain a minor bit of satisfaction by writing `wish-dreamweaver@macromedia.com`.

ALTERNATING ROW COLORS, THE TEMPLATE EXPRESSION WAY

Template expresssions are another nifty addition to template power in Dreamweaver MX. One extremely useful technique is establishing an alternating background color within a repeating region. After you've set up your repeating region in a template table, select the `<tr>` tag that repeats (you could also use a `<p>` tag) and enter Code view. Add this attribute to the tag:

```
bgcolor="@@((_index & 1) ?
'#FFFFFF' : '#FFFF99')@@"
```

This particular code will alternate a white and light yellow background; you can, of course, substitute any other color values you want. But what if you want to alternate every two rows or—heavens to Betsy!—every three rows? Change the number value included in the parentheses with the `_index` keyword (1 in the original code) to 2 or—gasp!— 4. (Caveat templator: Some higher values, such as 3 and 5, offer not such predictable results. Test thoroughly.)

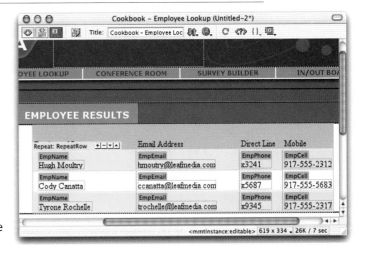

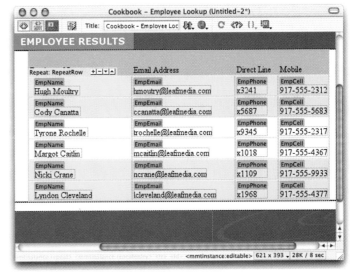

   THE HOBGOBLIN OF BIG MINDS

Often when updating a template in earlier versions of Dreamweaver, I'd find myself in a waking nightmare. Almost every time I did it, I either lost content and ended up with a wacky page because Dreamweaver could only insert content into one editable region. That's all changed in Dreamweaver MX, thanks to the Inconsistent Region Names dialog that is displayed whenever you're applying a new template to a page already based on a template and the regions do not match exactly,

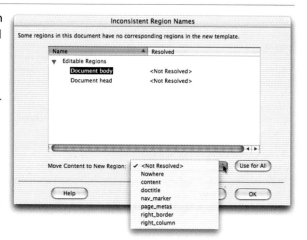

down to their case. You'll also see the dialog when you attempt to apply a template to a regular document. Through this interface, Dreamweaver gives you the chance to map the content in a document to any region in the template. If you realize you no longer need the content, you can discard it. You do, however, have to decide what to do with all the content; Dreamweaver refuses to budge until you make your choices clear.

   STYLIN' AT THE BIBLIOTECHIQUE

I love working with library items and style sheets. There is something so gratifying about dropping what appears to be a plain text element onto a page and, wham-o, you're looking good! Working the magic does take a fair degree of planning, however. Of primary importance is the need to make sure that the classes applied to your library item elements are included in your style sheet. Likewise, you want to be sure to define CSS rules for all the HTML tags used in the library items. One way to make sure that your bases are covered is to create the library item from a page where it is correctly styled. To keep you on your toes, Dreamweaver displays a warning that the style rules won't be included when you save the library item.

SHARING THE LIBRARY CARD

When working with library items, I often find that what works well in one site also can be used in another. Dreamweaver includes a rather zippy facility for just these occasions: Copy to Site. From the Library category of the Asset panel, first highlight the library items you want to copy, then select the Options menu and choose Copy to Site. Then, from the submenu, select the site to which you want to copy the library item. Be careful, though: only the library item itself is copied. Any dependent files on which the library item relies—such as images or Flash movies—need to be transferred manually.

   ## THE RE-ANIMATOR VISITS THE LIBRARY

I'm a big fan of anything that helps me correct a mistake I made—especially when it's a catastrophic one like deleting a library item. After a library item is gone, there's no way to update all the associated items spread throughout your site. Luckily, there is a way to bring that library item back from the dead. All you need to do is first locate an instance of the library item on a page and select it. Then, from the Property inspector, choose Recreate and Dreamweaver automagically restores the library item, down to the correct name. Feel free to do your Mad Scientist laugh after the operation is complete—I always do.

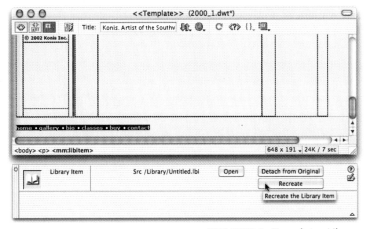

   SHHH! LIBRARY RULES!

As cool as library items are, they do have some limitations. The primary issue is that library items are decidedly restricted to the `<body>` of an HTML page—no `<head>` elements may apply. This means, first and foremost, that you can't make `<meta>` tags into library items. There are other ramifications, however. Although a library item can include a link that triggers a JavaScript behavior, custom JavaScript functions are not allowed. There is, however, a way around this limitation. With standard Dreamweaver behaviors, Dreamweaver automatically inserts the necessary JavaScript code into a page when a library item referencing that behavior is inserted. To get around the custom code limitation, use the Call JavaScript behavior to call the custom function. This is enough of an indication to Dreamweaver to insert your code along with the triggering library item.

   WHATEVER HAPPENED TO NEW FROM TEMPLATE...?

Back in the day of Dreamweaver 4, there was the File > New from Template command. Many have scoured the interface of MX to find out how to make a new child page from a template. I told you back in Chapter 1 that there are context menus all over the place in Dreamweaver, some of which offer options available only in those very context menus. New From Template is one of those instances where you won't find another menu command

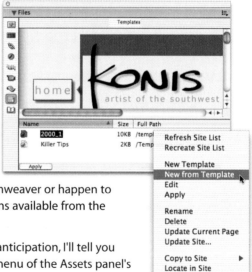

of its kind (unless you've customized Dreamweaver or happen to own my Template-Lover's Suite of extensions available from the `DWfaq.com` store...)

Now that I've built you up with just a little anticipation, I'll tell you that New From Template is in the context menu of the Assets panel's Templates category. Another way to create a new page based on a template is to select File > New and select the Templates tab to choose a template from the list of sites and generate the new template-based page. Both of the methods I just described will do; the latter method I find faster than waiting on the Assets panel to initialize. However, I find that the customized menu offers the fastest way, so if you're brave enough, I'll show you how to do that in Chapter 10.

ROLLOVER BEETHOVEN

You can swap as many images as you like on the single event, but bear in mind that they should be relatively close to the triggering hyperlink (otherwise, the swap may happen off-screen and go unseen by the user). Select the image or a hyperlink, click the Add (+) button on the Behaviors panel, and then

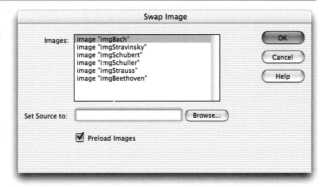

select the Swap Image behavior from the list.

If the list is filled with unnamed `<img>` elements, it will be difficult to determine which images are which so that you can apply the behavior. You may want to click Cancel, and go back and name all images that will be involved in the Property inspector by filling in the field to the left of the H (for height). Then go back to the Swap Image behavior dialog.

You can choose each listed image and then browse to the image you'd like replaced when the `onMouseOver` event is triggered. Each image that is affected by the behavior will have an asterisk beside it in the list.

   ## DOUBLE-CLICK AND FIX

When it comes time to make a change to a behavior—there always comes a time—you might be thinking that you'll have to remove the behavior and apply it again. That would be too much like work. Just locate the behavior in the Behaviors panel, and double-click the event you need to modify. Well, whadya know, the behavior's dialog appears with your current values set, allowing you to modify only the parameters you need to change and be done.

  NAVIGATION BARS MADE EASY

Adding images and their behaviors one by one to create an interactive navigation bar is a monotonous task. I tried doing this manually—before I discovered the easy way—and usually I made simple mistakes like not assigning the correct event to trigger an action. The Navigation Bar object (in the Common category of the Insert bar) speeds up the process dramatically by letting you add all the images and their behaviors in the same dialog. You can assign different images for Up, Over, Down, and Over While Down as well as choose a Horizontal or Vertical orientation. You can even decide to use tables or not to arrange the images that make up the navigation bar by indicating your preference in the Use Tables checkbox.

Picture a tabbed interface. Usually in this type of navigation bar, the tab is in its down state when you're viewing that tab's category. That's what the Show Down Image Initially checkbox option is all about. Using what you've learned in the "Double-Click and Fix" and "Rollover Beethoven!" tips within this chapter, you can create fancy navigation bars in a matter of a few minutes.

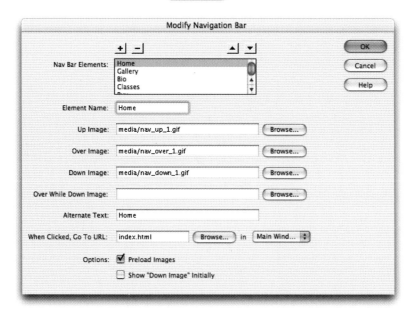

XHTML, THE WAVE OF THE FUTURE

As you may know, HTML 4.01 is the latest version of HTML and it is also the last version. HTML has been replaced with XHTML which isn't even a $1/4$ as scary as it may seem— especially with Dreamweaver's new XHTML features. If you're starting from scratch, XHTML is pretty easy because Dreamweaver will detect the XHTML doctype and make an effort to write compliant code. Using the File > Convert > XHTML command, you can give HTML documents a quick transformation to XHTML. After Dreamweaver has made the changes, you may be alerted that some images still need Alt text. You will have to add the Alt text manually. Now stick a bookmark in this page and then go read "Do You Validate?" in Chapter 9 to learn how to keep an eye on your code and make sure that it is valid.

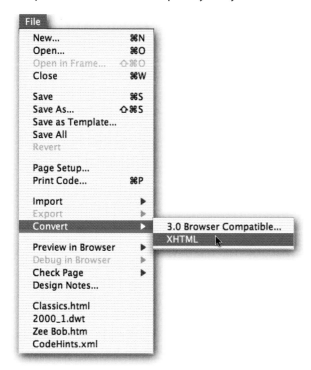

   LAYOUT VIEW WORDS OF WISDOM

Geared toward visual designers, Layout view allows you to draw tables in much the same way you would slice an image in an image editor like Fireworks. Creating code blindly, without knowing

what it does or whether it is correct is an easy way to get in trouble. Although Layout view has made many improvements in Dreamweaver MX, it isn't perfect. Never drag a table's border in Layout view or you run the risk of creating empty table cells, which in some browsers causes them to collapse and wreak havoc on your layout. The height attribute is invalid HTML and has a tendency to appear in table code created in Layout view. The best advice I can give for working in Layout view is to always work in Code and Design view so that you know what is going on with your code and only use it if you're well versed in HTML so that you can catch and correct the "gotchas" that are sometimes produced. Despite its flaws, Layout view can be great for quickly (in a matter of seconds) mocking up early design concepts that can be cleaned up later if needed.

   ON THIS DATE...

When you're unable to use server-side scripting to determine when a file was last modified, you can use Dreamweaver's Date object (located in the Common category of the Insert bar) to do this simply and effectively. This handy little object can update the page with the current date—and time, if you want it— of your computer's system clock. When you add the object you're given the

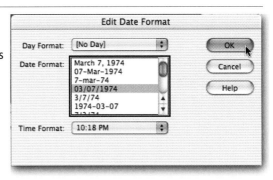

option to update the date each time you save the file. This functionality is controlled by the comment tags on each side of the date. If you're working in Code view, you can identify the comments by the `#BeginDate` and `#EndDate` before and after the date, respectively. Any CSS formatting other than the date or additional text, like `Last Modified On:`, should not be added between these tags or you risk breaking the functionality. If you're working in Design view and you select the date, Dreamweaver knows to include the comment tags in the selection so that you can add formatting or drag it anywhere you like on the page. If you need to change the actual date, you can do so only manually in Code view. To change the format, first select the date in Design view, and then click the Edit Date Format button on the Property inspector.

FLASH TEXT FOR MOCK UPS

If you've ever had a "client from hell" who wants to change every little thing at least 10 times before feeling satisfied, you're going to enjoy this tip. Next time you have a new site to develop for an indecisive client, try using the Flash Text object (found in the Media category of the Insert bar) to help you lay out a page. You can make a very graphical looking page with

rollovers using any font on your system without the need of an image editor. The dialog is truly simple, but be careful with the Apply button. After you press Apply, the .swf file is saved and you cannot use Ctrl+Z (Command+Z) to undo the changes.

When the client calls up and says, "Can you make the buttons bigger?" just click the resize handles and drag the Flash Text to the size you want. Changing the color, font, or rollover color is as easy as creating the Flash Text in the first place. Just double-click the Flash Text in Design view and the dialog you used to create the Flash Text appears so that you can make your changes. If the Property inspector isn't showing, the only way you can tell the difference between an image and Flash Text is to select the item and then see whether `<img>` or `<object>` is selected in the Tag Selector.

Maximum Acceleration

Two web developer guys meet for lunch one Tuesday afternoon. "I need a vacation. Everything lately has been work, work, work…", complains the first

Maximum Acceleration
dreamweaver tip variety pack

guy. The second guy says, "I know the feeling. I can't wait until next month. I'm going to Jamaica for a couple of weeks." The other developer responds, "Hey, that's not fair. You work on as many sites as I do. How can you afford to take the time off?" The second guy, looks down and notices Dreamweaver MX Killer Tips sticking out of his briefcase and quickly pushes the briefcase under the table and—with a very big grin—he then replies, "I must work faster than you do." During lunch, the first guy gripes about typical web development woes while the second guy just smiles and nods.

Hey, it could happen! This chapter is special—well they're all special but this one is different—because this chapter is like a box of chocolates. That's right, you never know what you're going to get. You just might find that perfect tip that you didn't even know you were looking for that frees up so much of your time that you can afford to take that vacation you've been wanting. You never know; stranger things have happened! Send me an email if you need a good travel agent…

BRINGING IN SEPARATE PARAGRAPHS FROM WORD

How many times has this happened to you? You highlight a bunch of paragraphs in Word and copy 'em. Switch to Dreamweaver and click paste. *Yikes!* All your nicely laid out paragraphs come in as one big block. Truth is, you haven't lost all your formatting— Dreamweaver interprets a single paragraph return as a line-break tag,
 . Two returns, however, are changed to paragraph tags. So the moral is this: If you're copying multiple paragraphs from your word processing document, make sure your paragraphs are separated by two returns.

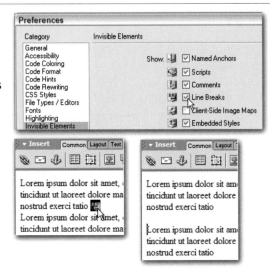

Bonus Tip! Change a <br> tag to a surrounding <p> in one move: With Invisible Elements turned on, select the <br> symbol and press Enter (Return)—the line-break is gone and the text is now wrapped in a paragraph tag.

   FOCUS YOUR ATTENTION RIGHT HERE

Here is a simple little JavaScript used to give a specific field focus in a form when the page is loaded so that the user can start filling out the fields right away. Right+click (Ctrl+click) the <body> tag in the Tag Selector in the lower left of the Document window if you're using Design view and choose Edit Tag (if you're in Code view, get ready to modify the <body> tag). Here's the code to add to the <body> tag:

```
onload="document.theFormName.theFieldName.focus();"
```

Replace theFormName with the exact name of your form and theFieldName with the exact name of the field in which you want the cursor to be positioned when the page loads. When I say exact, I mean it; make sure the casing is identical.

By the way, if an onload event is already present, you should add only the portion between the quotes and not a second onload attribute. Remember that functions must be separated by a semicolon, so if you put this at the start of an existing onload event you should be just fine.

WATCH OUT FOR KILLER OCTOTHORPES

How many times have you clicked on a link to a popup window and find that when you close the popup, you're back at the top of the page again? Well, you've been attacked by an octothorpe and I bet you didn't even know it! A *what-o-thorpe*, you ask? Octothorpe comes from the Greek word *octo*, which means eight. (If you've seen the movie *My Big Fat Greek Wedding*, you should know that all words come from a Greek word! Joe tells me that the *thorpe* part comes from James Oglethorpe, Georgia's founder. Should we believe him? The true origin is unkown according to the dictionary, so the world may never know…) Anyway, this is an

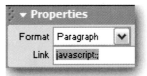

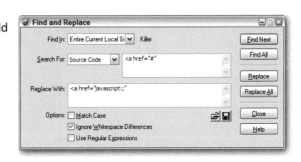

octothorpe: #. You can call it the number sign, a hash, a pound sign or any other words it may be known as, but I call 'em *octothorpes*.

Octothorpes are great for some things, but not for creating what is known as a *null link*. So as you use Dreamweaver's behaviors, keep an eye on the Link field of the Property inspector and make sure that you see `javascript:;` instead of an octothorpe. If you have a bunch of pages with null links you'd like to fix, you could use Dreamweaver's Find and Replace feature to search for this source code:

```
<a href=" #"
```

And then replace it with this:

```
<a href="javascript:;"
```

This way you'll never subject your site's visitors to killer octothorpes again.

 ## HEADING THIS WAY

Headings 1 through 6 in HTML are represented by <h1> through <h6> tags. To turn text into a heading, use Ctrl (Command)+1 through 6 to add the respective heading. Ctrl+Shift+P (Command+Shift+P) is used to make a paragraph and Ctrl+0 (Command+0) will remove any heading or paragraph formatting.

RESCALING AN IMAGE IN DREAMWEAVER

Here's one of the coolest tricks I know—if you've ever tried to rescale an image already in your web page, you're gonna love it too. You'll need Fireworks 3 or better to make it work, but this one technique is worth the price of the whole program. I'm sure you know that you can resize an image in Dreamweaver by dragging the lower-right corner, right? (Be sure to hold down the Shift key while dragging to keep the original height-to-width ratio.) Resizing an image this way is purely a

visual experience—and not a very good one at that. Dreamweaver is not a graphics editor, but it has a direct line to a great one: Fireworks. After you've resized the image so that it's picture perfect, choose Commands > Optimize Image in Fireworks. If you have the original PNG source file available, use it so that you get the best quality; but if not, a GIF or JPEG will work. When the Optimize Images dialog opens, switch to the File tab and presto! Your Dreamweaver-drawn dimensions are locked and loaded—all you need do is click the Update button and you're done. The Fireworks-in-Dreamweaver engine optimizes the graphic and replaces the original. You'll even find that the `<img>` tag includes the new width and height values. Schweeeet!

   QUICKLY CLEARING A PAGE

If you're like me, you try a slew of different layout designs before you find the right one. Here's a really fast way to scrap what you're doing and start over when you've got design fever: Just select `<body>` in the Tag Selector and press Delete. BAM! All the visible content—graphics, text, tables, Flash movies, what have you—is gone. A clean slate awaits your next masterpiece. Now this eradicates only the visible elements of a page; any code

in the `<head>`, such as the `<title>`, `<meta>` tags, or JavaScript functions, is untouched. You'll also find the `<body>` tag itself is unscathed, leaving any attributes or events as pristine as ever.

FINDING YOUR ASSETS IN A DARK ROOM (WITHOUT A FLASHLIGHT)

I just love dragging images, Flash movies, and library items from the Assets panel and dropping onto the page. Dreamweaver does a yeoman's job of keeping up with all the site elements, but it's not perfect by any means. Occasionally, you'll need to click the Refresh button to make Dreamweaver-imported assets appear. Should you ever feel the urge to copy over assets in some other fashion—like with a file manager—you'll need to take it one step further. Instead of simply clicking the Refresh button, Ctrl+click it (Command+click) and you'll trigger the Recreate Site List command. True, it might take a moment, but it's the one way to be sure you're seeing all your site assets. Okay, okay, there's another way—choose Recreate Site List from the Assets panel Options menu.

   ## EVERYBODY, COME ON AND DO DA COMBO, MON!

In a land of HTML forms, where every drop-down list is a what-you-see-is-all-you-get affair, a treat awaits you. A number of the dialog elements sprinkled throughout Dreamweaver are actually combo boxes—drop-down lists where you can type in your own values. In some instances, this feature is a quick way to choose a specific value. For example, if you haven't made the leap to CSS yet and are still using font size attributes, you don't have to go digging deep in the list to super-size a selection—just type 7 in the Size field of the Property inspector for instant gratification. On the flip side, the Link text field is also a combo box. Some folks forget that all those URLs they entered during the current Dreamweaver session are now available in handy-dandy list format, ready to be selected.

  CLOWNS TO THE LEFT OF ME, JOKERS TO THE RIGHT…

Even if your web page isn't filled with images of clowns and assorted jokers, you still can position your text so that it's "stuck in the middle" between two graphics. First, put your two images right next to each other on the page. Then, use the Property inspector to set the Align property of the one on the left to Left and—bet you saw this coming—the Align property for the one on the right to Right. Make sure you're using the Align drop-down list and not the align icons. Dreamweaver will instantly place the two graphics on opposing sides, leaving a very inviting empty space in the middle. Don't waste another second—fill that void with your (or your client's) golden words. This is great for those Greek column layouts you've been dying to do. If you've got Invisible Elements enabled, you might see a symbol representing the anchor points for one or

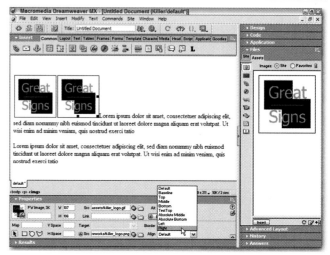

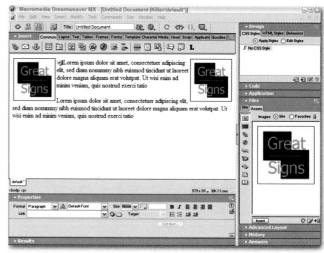

both `<img>` tags. They're safe to ignore (choose View > Visual Aids > Invisible Elements to hide them if you want), but don't delete them, whatever you do. If you zap 'em, your images will go too.

ZIPPY FORM ORGANIZATION WITH THE FIELDSET TAG

One of the keys to good design is proximity: Grouping related elements together makes it easier on the eye and the brain, especially when it comes to lengthy forms. The `<fieldset>` tag is a handy tool to keep in any form designer's palette. Supported by most modern browsers (Internet Explorer 5.0 and later and Netscape Navigator 6.0 and above),

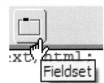

the `<fieldset>` tag groups elements by drawing a thin-lined box around them all and adding a legend in the top-left corner of the box. Address info—such as Street, City, State, Zip—is a likely target for a `<fieldset>` tag. It's a cool look and easy to do. To group existing form elements, go into Code view and select all the desired form elements. (When I've tried to do this in Design view, I've found Dreamweaver didn't always

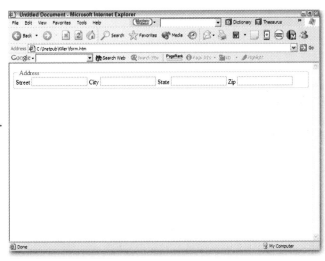

get all the necessary tags.) Then, from the Forms category of the Insert bar, choose the Fieldset object; you can either click it or drop it on the selection, and a small dialog prompts you for the fieldset legend. Both a `<fieldset>` and a `<legend>` tag are inserted, like this:

```
<fieldset>
 <legend>address</legend>
    <label>street <input type="text" name="street"></label>
    <label>city <input type="text" name="city"></label>
    <label>state <input type="text" name="state"></label>
    <label>zip <input type="text" name="zip"></label>
</fieldset>
```

The legend appears in Design view, but the box outline doesn't. Browser support does vary so be sure to preview in your favorite browser to see the results. Truly zippy.

WHERE, OH, WHERE HAVE MY WINDOW SIZES GONE?

If the key to being a successful real estate developer is location, location, location; for web-site developers, it's testing, testing, testing. One of the wide-ranging variances that design-ers face are different browser window sizes; you really don't know whether your audience is looking at your site with an window set at 640×480, 800×600, 1024×768 or something higher. Dreamweaver makes it easy to view your page in different dimensions by choosing the Window Size pop-up on the status bar. It's a pretty nifty feature—sometimes, however, you'll try to use it and none of the options in the list are active. In Windows, Dreamweaver automatically disables the feature whenever your Document window is maximized. To restore the options, back off the maximized state by selecting the Restore Down button on Windows systems.

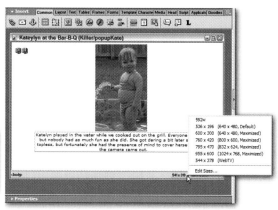

STAYING IN GOOD FORM

Naming conventions are extremely helpful in avoiding common form-processing errors. The trick is to create unique labels for form

elements that are instantly identifiable to the developer. My technique is to combine the type of form element with its purpose. For example, I would call a text field for accepting the name of a country countryText—whereas a list element for the same purpose would be countryList. I use mixed case (also known as *intercapping*) to avoid spaces—a definite no-no in web naming—but this helps keep it legible.

PLAYING NICE WITH THE INSERT BAR

Looking for a little more flexibility in your Dreamweaver workspace? By default, the Insert bar (previously known as the Objects panel in earlier versions of Dreamweaver), is all by its lone-some. But it doesn't have to remain unattached. When you're working in the Dreamweaver MX workspace or HomeSite/Coder Style workspace, you can drag it down to the extended Property inspector by the gripper (those tiny little dots to the left of the Panel group name) and free up the top part of the screen. Or you can swing the other way and bring the Property inspector up to the Insert bar's neck of the woods. You cannot, however, dock the Insert bar (or the Property inspector for that matter) with any of the other Panel groups that are on the side of the workspace. On the other hand, the Insert bar and Property inspector can be docked with a Panel group that is floating footloose and fancyfree.

   ### "A" IS FOR ACCESSIBLE APPLETS

If you're into Java applets, you're probably aware that you can enter a URL or path to a graphic as the Alt attribute and the image will be displayed for users with Java disabled. Dreamweaver even provides a Browse for File icon next to the Alt field on the Property inspector to aid your picture pickin'. But Section 508 guidelines dictate that every non-text element must have a text equivalent—so how do you

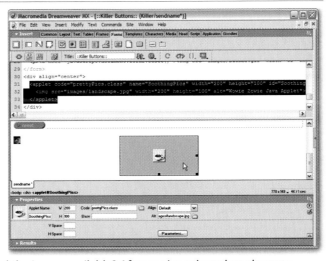

make both alternative text and the image available? After you've selected an alternate image, Dreamweaver inserts an `<img>` tag within the `<applet>` tag. In Code view, add an alt attribute, like `alt="Wowie Zowie Java Applet"`, to the `<img>` tag. Now, you've got the best of all worlds.

   MULTIPLYING RADIO BUTTONS

The new Radio Group object in the Forms category of the Insert bar is a good all-in-one interface for making sure that all your radio buttons are properly named. There's another technique, however, honed from the ol' days when we didn't have such new-fangled doo-dads. It starts by creating a single radio button and giving it whatever group name you desire. Next, copy and paste as many copies of the button as you need; a really fast way to do this is to Ctrl+drag (Opt+drag) out the copies. The radio group name will be the same for all your copies. All you have to do is make sure the values are unique and select which one of the radio buttons, if any, is checked.

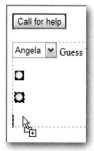 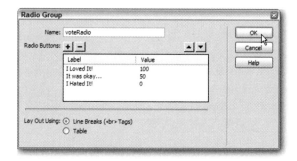

   FANCY-SCHMANCY FORM BUTTONS

Looking to spice up a boring form? A common element to all forms is the Submit button—and its standard appearance is definitely commonplace. You can replace the ordinary gray button with a graphic button in one of two ways. If your form has only a Submit button, with no reset or other type of button, you can use an image field. You can add an input image using the Image Field object found in the Forms category of the Insert bar. When users select an image field (that's inside a form), the form is automatically submitted. There is a drawback to using
image fields—you can't use them for other purposes, like resetting a form. The second method uses JavaScript. In this technique, you bring in a regular image to act as your Submit button and give it a link like this: `javascript:document.form1.submit()`, assuming that your form is named `form1`. If you want to use another graphic to clear a form, just change the link to `javascript:document.form1.reset()`. Not only do these types of buttons display the pointing hand icon, but you could also include rollover images if you like.

LABEL-LICIOUS

The new accessibility options for form elements, which can be enabled in Preferences, include a rather cool feature— labels. Supported in the latest browsers, the <label> tag makes it easy to associate any form element with specific text, which appears normally but can also be noted by screen readers. The Input Tag Accessibility Attributes dialog gives you two possible

routes to take when creating labels. Use the Wrap with Label Tag when your form element and label are side-by-side; this gives you code like this:

```
<label>First Name<input type="text" name="firstnameText"></label>
```

If you prefer to separate the label and form element into separate columns, use the Attach Label Tag Using 'for' Attribute option. This choice results in code like this:

```
<label for="firstnameText">First Name</label>
<input type="text" name="firstnameText" id="firstnameText">
```

   BUTTON, BUTTON, WHO'S GOT THE BUTTON?

Form buttons aren't just for submitting or resetting forms—they can be pressed into a multitude of services. If you need an instantly recognizable button to trigger any function, the form button is ideal; you don't even need to put it within a <form> tag. The easiest way to assign a function directly to a button is to use the Quick Tag Editor. Select the button and press Ctrl+T (Command+T) to display the <input> tag. Tab to the end of the tag and enter onClick="doMyFunction()" where doMyFunction() is the name of…well, your

custom JavaScript function. For simple JavaScript commands like alerts, you can enter the JavaScript directly, like this:

```
onClick="javascript:alert('Call 555-1234 for help.')"
```

ANCHORS AWAY

Let your visitors jump to the right spot on your web page by using what is known as a *named anchor*. You can drop an anchor on your page using the Named Anchor object found in the Common Category of the Insert bar. Give the anchor a name that is alphanumeric—lowercase, no spaces, and not starting with a number. As long as Invisible Elements are enabled (View > Visual Aids > Invisible

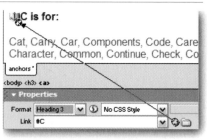

Elements should be checked), you will see a little anchor icon on your page. You can click and drag the icon to wherever you want in the document. You can save yourself not only time, but typos too, if you use the point-to-file method to link to your named anchors. To manually link to a named anchor, add an octothorpe to the end of the filename plus the name you gave the anchor. For example:

```
<a href="default.asp#backToTop">:: Back To Top ::</a>
```

BYE, BYE HELPER TEXT

Sometimes it is necessary to have a form field already filled out so users understand what they are supposed to enter. The only problem with this method is that it means the users have to delete the pre-filled entry themselves, which can be annoying—especially if there are many fields to clear. You can make it easier by clearing the text for them with some easy JavaScript. To clear an `<input>` tag's value, add the following:

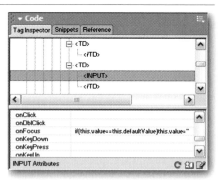

```
onfocus="this.value=''"
```

You wouldn't want to clear the form every time the user clicks inside it because that could really get annoying. Let's clear the field only if the default value specified by the `value` attribute of the `<input>` tag is present, by using this code instead:

```
onfocus="if(this.value==this.defaultValue)this.value=''"
```

A great way to add this code is by first clicking on the field in Design view to select it, and then adding the value to the `onFocus` attribute in the Tag inspector.

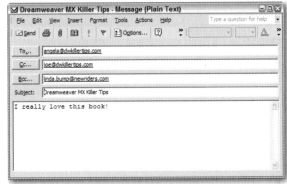

THAT'S WHAT IT'S ALL ABOUT

A clear subject line in an email can be very helpful to the recipient, but often the sender isn't specific enough. There's no guarantee that the user won't modify the subject line you create for them, but it doesn't hurt to try! Use the Email Link object (found in the Common category of the Insert bar) and in the E-mail field, enter the following:

```
you@yourwebsite.com?subject=
The%20Subject%20Here
```

Spaces in the subject must be encoded with %20 and any other special characters must be encoded as well. You can make use of additional attributes and values, such as cc (Carbon copy), bcc (Blind Carbon Copy), and body (the message) by stringing them together using an ampersand as in the following code (which should appear all on the same line in Code view):

```
angela@dwkillertips.com?subject=Dreamweaver%20MX%20Killer%20Tips&cc=
joe@dwkillertips.com&bcc=linda.bump@newriders.com&body=I really love
this book!
```

JAVASCRIPT REQUIRED

You never know when users have fiddled with their browser settings and decided to disable JavaScript. The `<noscript>` tag will let you present those users with a special message only for them. Switch to the Script category of the Insert bar and

then click in the body of the document where you want the message to display—near the top is usually a good spot so that it is seen the moment the page is loaded. Click the noscript icon—the one in the middle—and the Tag Editor dialog will appear. If you've never used the `<noscript>` tag, you may want to click Tag Info in the lower right of the dialog to display a description and example of the `<noscript>` tag. Enter your message in the text area and if you'd like, switch to the Style Sheet/Accessibility category on the left, fill out the values on the right, and then click OK.

   TRANSFERING SITES

Do you have a client or co-worker using Dreamweaver? You can save them the time of defining a site by exporting your site definition for them to import. This very method is how you'll transfer sites between your own computers. Select Site > Edit Sites and then click the site you want to export. Click the Export button and continue with the export—I'm sure you can figure it out. Do the same for each site definition—it is good to have a backup of all site definitions, just in case. In fact, set this book down—but keep it open of course—and export all of your defined sites right now. It is a known issue that without rhyme or reason, the site definitions may be lost completely.

It is important to realize that the .ste files store all the info in the Site Definition dialog but it does not back up the files on your site. You'll need to do that manually. If you opted to include the password in the .ste, be aware that though it is encrypted it is conceivable that it can be deciphered. Give the .ste files to your client or co-worker so that they can use the Import button on the Edit Sites dialog to import the site definition.

   NO MORE BROKEN LINKS

You are not only able to find broken links, but you can also find orphaned files—those are files not used within the site at all. While at least one document in your site is open, select Window > Results > Link Checker or use the keyboard shortcut Ctrl+Shift+F9 (Command+Shift+F9) and then click the green arrow icon on the left to select Check Links for Entire Site or one of the other two choices. When the command is finished, if any links are broken, they'll be listed in the panel. Click the filename in the Broken Links column and you can edit the link or browse to the file. Dreamweaver will even ask whether you'd like to update any other broken references to the same file. After those bad links are fixed, they are removed from

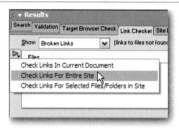

the list. In the top left of the panel, you can choose to show external and orphaned files. No matter what you're displaying, double-clicking a file listed on the left in the panel will open it in Dreamweaver for editing.

REUSABLE JAVASCRIPT

Whenever you have JavaScript code that is common to more than one page, you should externalize the code to its own file and link it to the document(s) that need it. A blank file with the script added to it minus the `<script>` tags and saved with the .js file extension is all you need. When it comes time to link the external JavaScript file to a document, go to the Scripts category of the Assets panel. Clicking the filename will reveal the file's code inside the preview area. You can either drag the file by its name into the document or click the Insert icon in the lower left of the Assets panel. The `<script>` tag is added to the document with the proper `src` attribute that points to the JavaScript file. You should add a `type` attribute to the `<script>` tag if you want to be sure your page uses valid (X)HTML.

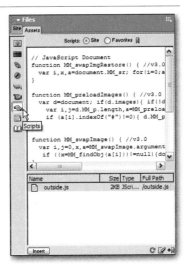

   VIEW AS ROOT

A site map can get rather large and difficult to view. When this happens, you'll know just what to do. You can right-click (Ctrl+click) any other file in the Site Map—as long as it resides locally—and choose View As Root. After doing so, you'll notice that the Site Navigation display has added an arrow followed by a filename for every file in the path to the file being viewed as the root. Clicking any of the files listed in the Site

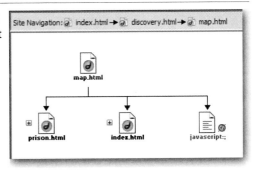

Navigation crumb trail will update the site map to use that file as its root. If you haven't set a home page for your site or if you need to change the current one, you can right-click (Ctrl+Click) a file in the Local Files section of the Site panel and choose Set as Home Page from the context menu.

INITIALLY SELECTED VALUE

After inserting a List/Menu object, you can add the possible values for the form element by clicking the List Values button in the Property inspector. After

you've added all the item's labels and values, click OK. You'll probably want to choose one of the values to be pre-selected. You can do this by clicking the label in the Initially Selected field in the lower portion of the Property inspector. One day I decided to remove the Initially Selected value so that nothing was shown in the list by default. To my surprise, when I clicked in the Initially Selected field of the Property inspector, it seemed impossible. I thought I was stuck with my choice unless I went into Code view to do the change manually. Now I know that if I Ctrl+click (Command+click) the selected value, it becomes unselected.

REQUIRING INPUT

Making sure that a user has completed a form correctly is made easy with the Check Form behavior. The Check Form behavior will let you specify which fields are required and you can choose the type of user input, such as email address, a number, or within a range

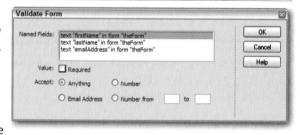

of numbers. After you've established a form with one or more text fields or text areas, use the Tag Selector to select the form tag. Now click the Add (+) button on the Behaviors panel and choose Validate Form near the bottom of the drop-down list. When the dialog appears, select the form field in the list and choose the appropriate values for the remaining options. You may do this for each of the fields listed in the dialog.

By applying the behavior to the `<form>` tag, the validation occurs at the time the user submits the form. If the requirements are met the form is submitted, otherwise the user will get a JavaScript alert letting them know what fields need to be corrected. If you want the validation to take place while the user is filling out the form and proceeds to the next field apply the behavior to each text field element rather than to the `<form>` tag.

Greased Lightning

Deadlines, we've all got 'em—even me.
Right now I'm thinking, "What the heck
can I say about building dynamic
applications that is funny for Chapter 8's

Greased Lighting
application building tips

intro?" as my deadline quickly approaches.
So I turned to my good friend Dan Short for
inspiration. We were already chatting along
when I said, "Tell me something funny about
building dynamic sites."

I barely blinked twice before Dan replied,
"There are some hidden costs to developing
dynamic sites that most people don't think of.
You'll need additional equipment, such as
beer, pizza, thicker glasses, and hair coloring
for the gray spots. After you have these initial
supplies in order you'll be ready to dig in."

Of course I replied, "LMAO, I'm stealing this
from you for the book with credit <smiley>. Is
there anything else funny I can permanently
borrow from you for the book?"

"Dreamweaver wouldn't be the product it
is without Dan... just think about it. Who else
would make a blog that yellow? That alone
has boosted sales immeasurably, but no one
will ever know…" So there you have it folks,
Mr. Daniel W. Short's words of wisdom.
(For more of Dan's wisdom, see his blog:
http://blog.web-shorts.com) Thanks, Dan!

I know that diving into building dynami-
cally driven sites can be intimidating. But
don't worry; you're about to learn all you
never knew but were afraid to ask…

   SAFER INCLUDES

One of the beauties of creating dynamic sites is the ability to take advantage of server-side includes. Similar to an external JavaScript file, the code calls the file to be included on a page. When an update is needed, only the single include file needs be updated and uploaded to affect all files that reference it. The biggest mistake you can make using includes is one you may never have considered: your file-naming convention. Many developers like to use an .htm or .inc file extension to help them easily identify the files as an include file. Although it is acceptable to use .inc or .htm as file extensions, if they are found on the server, they could expose server-side code that you would not want users to have access to. Either be certain that these files do not contain server-side code, or use your server-language's file extension (.asp, .cfm, .php, etc.) for the include files. To help you identify the files easily in your site as includes, you may want to put all of your include files in a folder called includes or name the files with an inc_ prefix.

   PRE-FILLED FORMS

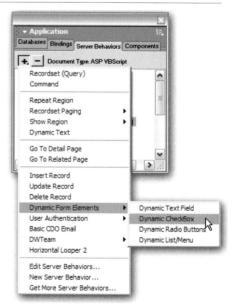

You've laid out a really nice contact form, but you'd like to have it filled out already with some dynamic values from a recordset. The fastest way to do this for text fields is to click-n-drag the recordset field directly onto the text field in Design view. For checkboxes, lists, and radios, you'll want to use the Dynamic Form Elements submenu choices.

FINDING YOUR WAY DOWN THE PATH

The toughest part of getting started with an ASP site is making the connection to the database. This is especially difficult if you don't know the server's path to the database file so that you can make your connection. To keep users from being able to browse to the database file on the web, a database should be stored a level above the root of the site. (If your host does not allow the database to be stored above your site's root, they may provide an alternatively protected directory that cannot be browsed from the web.) To get the path to the database file, you need to know the name of the folder in which the file is stored as well as the filename. On any ASP page, somewhere in the code after the <body> tag, add:

```
<%= Server.MapPath("..\databaseFolder\theDatabase.mdb") %>
```

You should, of course, replace the part inside the quotation marks with your own information. When you preview the page, you'll get a full path to the file shown in the browser, which will look something like this:

```
D:\aFolder\wwwroot\yourSite\databaseFolder\theDatabase.mdb
```

Now you've got the path; next comes success.

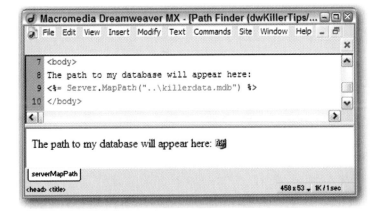

CELLULAR INSURANCE

Insuring your cell phone against loss or theft is a good tip, but instead let's talk about ensuring that table cells have content. You already know that Netscape 4.x can have conniptions when a cell is left totally empty. You also know that if a table has a border set, empty cells don't get the border and it looks terrible in Internet Explorer. When you're dealing with a dynamically driven website, there is often the chance that some of the fields in the database won't return any data. When this happens and there aren't any other contents in a table cell, you could end up with a totally empty cell if a record is not returned. We can't have that, now can we? Using an if/else statement, you can determine if a field is not empty the record should be shown; otherwise, show a non-breaking space or a display message you've entered—just don't let that cell stay empty. Here's some sample ColdFusion code for you to chew on:

```
ColdFusion:
<cfif recordset.theField NEQ "">
<cfoutput>#recordset.theField#</cfouput>
<cfelse>
 
</cfif>
```

and sample code for you if you use ASP/VBScript:

```
<% If recordset("theField ") <> "" Then %>
<%= recordset("theField ") %>
<% Else %>
 
<% End If %>
```

You'll find objects in the Insert bar to help you write your if/else statements in a category for the current document's server model; for example, CF Flow for .cfm files or ASP for .asp files.

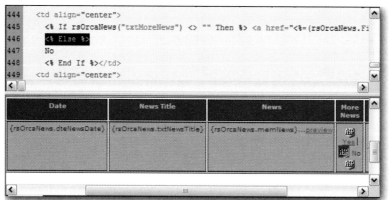

GOOD HABITS ARE HARD TO COME BY

Usually I tend to pick up my friends' bad habits, but this time I picked up a really good one. Setting up a good set of naming conventions can really make programming easier. Let's start with how we name database fields. I like to give each field an intuitive name with a two or three letter prefix that tells me what type of field it is in the database: mem (Memo), dte (Date), int (Integer or Number), and txt (Text). For 1/0, yes/no, true/false type fields you can use bit (think binary storage) or bol (Boolean). So let's suppose that the field I'm working with is a memo type; my field would be named memTheNews. When it comes to recordsets, I like to prefix them all with rs, as in rsTheNews. Did you notice that I just used TheNews for both memTheNews and rsTheNews? While I'm coding, I can spot that one is a recordset and the other is a memo type field, but more importantly, I never end up with naming conflicts.

   DOUBLE-CLICK AND FIX TOO

When it comes time to make a change to a server behavior—there always comes a time—you might be thinking that you'll have to remove the server behavior and apply it again. (This is starting to sound exactly like "Double-Click and Fix" in Chapter 6, isn't it?) That would be too much like work. Just locate the server behavior in the panel, and double-click the event you need to modify. Well, whadya know, the server behavior's dialog appears with your current values set, allowing you to modify only the parameters you need and be done. But wait, there's more—you also can do this with recordsets

that are listed in the Bindings or Server Behaviors panels. If you ever spot a red exclamation mark next to a recordset or server behavior, use this double-click and fix method. Usually it is as simple as showing the dialog and clicking OK. If you like to hack server behavior output to suite your needs, you'd better read the tip later in this chapter, called "That's My Code, No Touchy."

   REUSING MEMO TYPE FIELDS

With ColdFusion, you can use a field as many times as you'd like for display or for if statements; it doesn't matter. On the other hand, ASP is a little more finicky when it comes to reusing memo type fields. Let's say that you want to check to see whether a memo type field in the database is empty, and if it is, you want to display a message to the user. Then later on the same page you want to put the same memo field in another location. You're gonna' get errors, bubba, or no data—depending on what you're trying to do. When you need to reuse a memo field, the way to get it working is to assign the memo field's value to a variable, and then call that variable whenever you need it. Take this, for example:

```
<% Dim myMemoFieldVariable
myMemoFieldVariable =
rsMyRecordset.Fields.Item("memMyActualMemoField").value
%>
```

Now whenever you need to display the variable, it would be done like so:

```
<%= myMemoFieldVariable %>
```

Remember that you must declare the variable before you try to use it in the page, or it won't work!

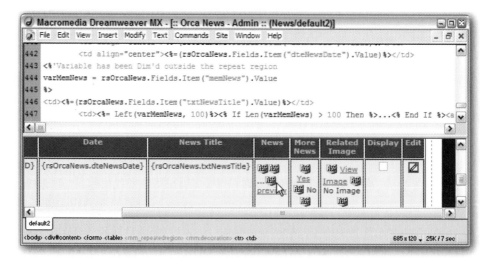

REUSING RECORDSETS

Everybody has done this…make a page, save it as a
different page, strip out what you don't need, save
again, and continue working. Well, if you're doing
that just so you don't have to recreate a complicated
recordset, don't bother with that tired old method.
Just right-click (Control+click) the recordset and
select Copy; then right-click (Control+click) again
in either the Server Behavior or Bindings panel and
select Paste. You can paste in a new document's
Server Behaviors or Bindings panel, but if you paste
the recordset you copied in the same document,
Dreamweaver gives the recordset a new name. If
you're doing that, I assume it is because you're going
to modify that recordset because you shouldn't ever
need the same exact recordset twice. ColdFusion
users enjoy being able to use a field as many times as
they'd like, but if you're using ASP and have emptied
a recordset, you may be tempted to define an identical one. Don't give in to that temptation; just add

`<% rsMyRecordsetNameHere.MoveFirst() %>`

to the page before the second usage of the recordset
and that will get you back to the start of your recordset again.

 THAT'S MY CODE, NO TOUCHY

Dreamweaver tries to be helpful whenever possible, but when I write my own server-side code I don't want anyone touching it—no matter how good their intentions—without me knowing about it. Play it safe, and make sure that the Code Rewriting preference is set to Never Rewrite Code in Edit > Preferences (Dreamweaver > Preferences on Mac OS X). There are exceptions to this rule; despite this setting, code can be re-written. Usually this happens when you've

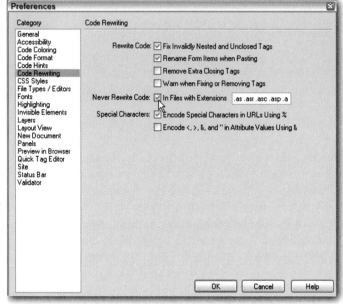

hand-coded and modified a server behavior. If you need to update the code of a server behavior you've modified, it is safest that you do it manually and not using the previously mentioned "Double-Click and Fix Too" trick. If you often find yourself modifying Dreamweaver server behaviors manually, you may want to check out "Rated X: Macromedia Code Exposed" in Chapter 10.

FORMAT THAT DATA

I've formatted data in UltraDev, but the first time I went
to do it in Dreamweaver MX, I was lost. For a moment
I thought that Macromedia had moved formatting
options elsewhere, but after a few minutes I realized that
I can still use the Bindings panel to format data just like
before. To get to the all-powerful Format column, you
may have to use the horizontal scrollbar at the bottom
of the panel. Yeah, I missed that too. I adjusted the width
of the Format column in my Bindings panel so that I
wouldn't need to scroll by clicking and dragging the
border between the Format and the Binding column.
Now all you need to do is click an inserted field or insert
one in Design view, and then you can click the drop-
down arrow that lets you choose from a whole bunch of
server formats to pretty up that data.

   NOW YOU SEE IT, NOW YOU DON'T

I've found a lot of
uses for the series
of Show Region
server behaviors;
being able to con-
ditionally display an

area of the page adds a lot of power to my application. You need to take special care, however, when applying one of the Show Region server behaviors that react when either the
first or last record of a recordset is called: Show If First Record, Show If Not First Record,
Show If Last Record, or Show If Not Last Record. Before you can implement any of these four
server behaviors, you need to make sure that one of the Recordset Paging server behaviors
has already been applied to the page. The Recordset Paging server behaviors also are
known as Move To Record server behaviors, because that's their job—to move to the first,
last, next, or previous record or to a specific record. Dreamweaver depends on variables
from the Move To Record server behaviors to make the Show Region server behaviors work.

CHAPTER 8 • Application Building Tips　**159**

   ROLLOVER, FIDO1; ROLLOVER, FIDO2

Although it's most common to see text fields be a part of a repeat region, you can, of course, include images. Many result pages from a catalog search include both a text and visual description of the items sought after. Now, let's say you want to get really fancy and add rollover effects to those images. Sounds simple enough, right? You just assign a Swap Image behavior and specify a data field from your recordset as the `src` attribute for the second image. Unfortunately, the Swap Image behavior won't work without tweaking the image name (not the `src`) to make it unique for every item. Here's what the original rollover code looks like:

```
<A HREF="#" onMouseOut="MM_swapImgRestore()" onMouseOver="MM_swapImage
➡('Image1','','<%=(rsCat.Fields.Item("imageover").Value)%>',0)">
<IMG NAME="Image1" BORDER="0" SRC="<%=(rsCat.Fields.Item
➡("image").Value)%>">
```

To get a rollover to work, you'll need to append an incrementing variable to the name attributes so that each image in the repeat region is unique, like this ASP code (the added code is in bold):

```
<A HREF="#" onMouseOut="MM_swapImgRestore()" onMouseOver="MM_swapImage
➡('Image<%=Repeat1__numRows%>','','<%=(rsCat.Fields.Item
➡("imageover").Value)%>',0)">
<IMG NAME="Image<%=Repeat1__numRows%>" BORDER="0"
SRC="<%=(rsCat.Fields.Item("image").Value)%>">
```

ColdFusion users can use the `#CurrentRow#` attribute to get the same effect.

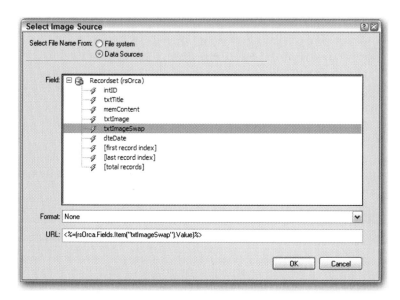

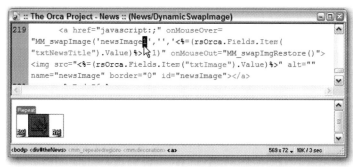

CHAPTER 8 · Application Building Tips   **161**

YES, WE HAVE NO RECORDS TODAY

A results page for the standard search application is generally set up to handle any number of items—some even use recordset navigation so that users can page through the results. However, what if there are no matches to the search criteria? Do you really want a "Now showing 0 of 0 records" message on the screen? Of course you don't! You want something kind, but firm, like, "No matches. Try again. Loser." With the use of two standard server behaviors, you can hide unnecessary elements and simultaneously show your message. To hide your recordset navigation (and anything else unwanted), select the undesired elements and apply the Show If Recordset Not Empty server behavior. This will hide the region when no results are found. Next, add your "No Records Found" message (or a Flash sound file that gives 'em the raspberry), select it, and then apply Show If Recordset Is Empty. Presto-chango—two completely different looks to handle any search results situation.

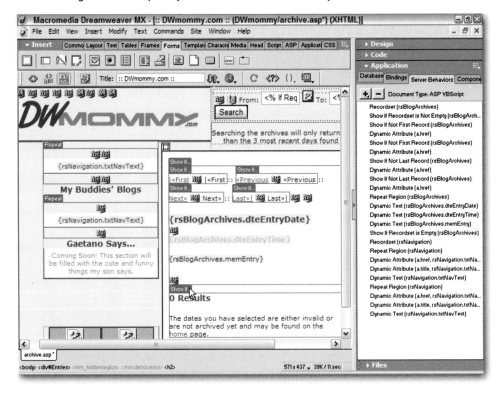

COPING WITH LOGIN FAILURE

I'm not a big fan of Sorry pages, are you? You know, you attempt to log in to an application and clumsy-finger-itis strikes and you mistype your user name or password. Suddenly you're faced with a some variation of an entire HTML page devoted to telling you that you've failed and you should click the back button to give it another go. There's got to be a better way—and I'm here to give it to you.

The beauty of this approach is that it uses the standard Dreamweaver Log In User server behavior and one little bit of extra code. First, apply your Log In User server behavior normally; in the If Log In Fails, Go To field of the dialog, replace the URL to your "I'm sorry" page with an address like this: `login.asp? failed=true`, where `login.asp` (or `login.cfm`) is the current login page. This will redisplay the login screen, giving folks a chance to re-enter their info without having to engage the Back button. Next, wherever you'd like your error message to appear to inform the user of the failed login attempt, add ASP code like this:

```
<%if (cStr(Request("failed"))<>"") then Response.Write("The username or
password entered is not valid.  Please try again.")%>

The ColdFusion version of this code would look like this:<cfif IsDefined
➥("URL.failed")><cfoutput>The username or password entered is not valid.
Please try again.</cfoutput></cfif>
```

Feel free to make your error message as uplifting or disparaging as you like.

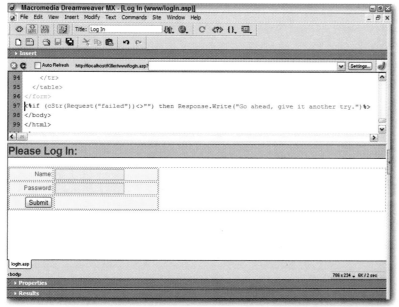

   BASIC (SQL) TRAINING

You don't know, but you've been told: SQL's hard to learn it cold. Let Dreamweaver be your personal drill instructor. When building recordsets, Dreamweaver offers both a Simple and an Advanced interface. You can pick up a great deal of SQL syntax simply by switching between the two. First, create a recordset in Dreamweaver's Simple Recordset dialog. Start off really basic and just choose a table in a data source while

accepting all the other defaults. Now, select Advanced and you'll see the corresponding SQL statement. Choose Simple to return to the other interface and make a single change—for example, you might change the Columns option from All to Selected, and then choose a couple of columns. Return to the Advanced interface and see how the SQL statement has been modified. Try adding a filter next; there's much to explore in this area and you'll begin to see how variables are declared and incorporated into the SQL statement. Make sure to select Test from time to time to see the results of your query.

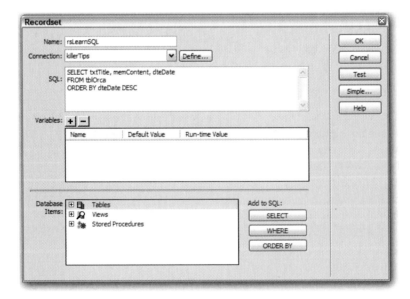

VIEWS FROM AFAR

Views give you another way of incorporating more
powerful SQL statements with a minimum of pain.
A *view* is a virtual table that combines columns from
related tables; in Access, views are called *queries*.
Access makes it fairly easy to create complex SQL

statements—just pick the columns from the tables you want to include and, assuming that
the tables are related by a key field, Access writes the SQL statement for you. When creating a
recordset, Dreamweaver lists all the views it finds in a data source along with the tables. Select
a view just as you would a table—and then you can choose which columns to include, which
filter to apply, and how to sort it. One little trick to keep in mind: if you don't see a particular
view listed in the simple Recordset dialog, scroll down the list. Dreamweaver displays all the
tables first in alphabetical order, followed by all the views, also in alphabetical order.

HIGHLIGHTING THE DYNAMIC

When you insert a dynamic text element onto a page,
Dreamweaver displays both the recordset and the
field name in curly braces, like this:`{ employees.
employeesID }`. To differentiate the dynamic text
from standard text, Dreamweaver also highlights
the element using the Translated color selected
in the Highlighted category of Preferences.

By default, Dreamweaver uses the same color
for editable regions and third-party tags;
you're free to adjust the highlight color if you
want your dynamic text to stand out more.
If you don't want to see the highlight at all,
toggle off View > Visual Aids > Invisible
Elements. (Instead of going through the
menus, I prefer to use the View Options
button on the Document toolbar to choose
Visual Aids > Invisible Elements.) Should
the dynamic text element names prove
too distracting because of their length,
you can reduce them to just the curly braces
by selecting the Show Dynamic Text As {}
option in the Invisible Elements category
of Preferences.

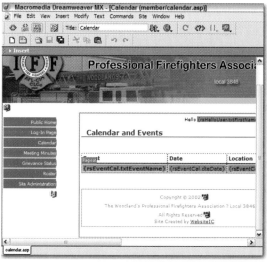

GETTING IT RIGHT FROM THE DATA SOURCE

Creating data-driven pages is like coming down a ladder—miss that first step and you're in for an unwelcome surprise. A data-driven page really starts with the proper formulation of the data itself. Let's look at three areas often misunderstood by web application newbies who are dealing with text, links, and images. First, text is far more flexible in databases than is commonly assumed. For example, a memo field in Access (used when the data runs longer than 255 characters), also can hold HTML tags; so you could store—and retrieve—multiple paragraphs with full formatting. When working with data that will be included as links, you might be tempted to set the data field to a Hyperlink type. Hyperlink styled data looks real pretty in Access but is completely useless in Dreamweaver; store your linking data as straight text instead. With images, it's best just to save just the filename and not the path to the image. If you want to include dynamic images located in a separate folder, choose Insert > Image and then choose the Select File Name From Data Source option. Select the proper field and, in the URL field, prepend the desired path (in other words, add the path before the code). For example, an ASP final URL might resemble this code:

```
images/thumbs/<%=(employees.Fields.Item("images").Value)%>
```

The ColdFusion code is different, even though the concept remains the same:

```
images/thumbs/<cfoutput>#employees.images#</cfoutput>
```

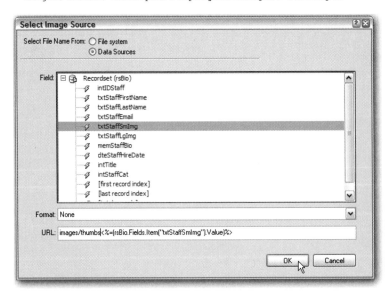

NOW THAT'S REFRESHING

So you're working in Live Data view, enjoying the fact that Dreamweaver lets your design your page with actual data shown, and you change the color of one of the dynamic text fields—but none of the other data in the repeat region changes. What's up with that? You've got Auto-Refresh enabled: why doesn't it automatically refresh? The Auto-Refresh option only updates the page when a change is made server-side—and text color changes (whether via HTML or CSS) are definitely client-side. To propagate a client-side change, select the Refresh icon on the Live Data toolbar. To see the Auto-

Refresh option in action, change the format of a selected dynamic text element from the Format column of the Bindings panel. You could, for example, specify the AlphaCase to be Upper and all the dynamic text entries would be displayed in uppercase after Dreamweaver detects the format change and automatically refreshes the page.

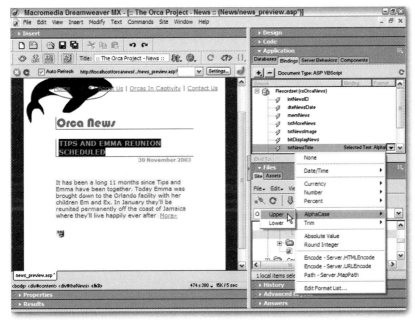

  CUSTOM RECORDSET NAVBAR

When you are building
a page that displays
a lot of data-driven
entries, recordset
navigation is often
essential. When you
use recordset naviga-

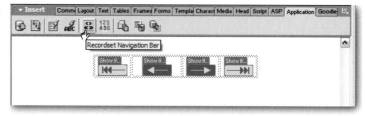

tion, Dreamweaver provides almost instant gratification. Choose the Insert > Application
Objects > Recordset Navigation Bar and Dreamweaver provides a complete navigation aid.
In addition to inserting eight separate server behaviors, Dreamweaver adds either text or
images to create links to the next, previous, first and last set of records. Naturally, you can
style the text however you like, but what if you'd prefer to use custom images instead of the
Macromedia inserted ones? If you're using the Recordset Navigation Bar throughout your
site, replace the source images found in the Dreamweaver MX/Configuration/Shared/
UltraDev/Images folder: first.gif, last.gif, next.gif, and previous.gif. By replacing the source
images, Dreamweaver will use your custom images instead of the standard ones.

   TESTING, TESTING

I'm really pretty enamored of the Live Data view and not just because of its considerable
coolness factor, either. I've found numerous web applications where I can use Live Data
view—and specifically, the URL parameter field—to field test my application. Before Live
Data view came on the scene, I checked any web application which incorporated a URL
parameter (that is, http://www.idest.com/extensions.asp?id=341) by entering various values
in a browser and, if there were any problems with spacing or layout, opened the page in
Dreamweaver and made corrections—then retested it in the browser. Live Data view and
the URL parameter field cuts out the middle man and allows me to enter my values directly
in Dreamweaver and immediately make any necessary changes. However, there have been
times when I get an error stating that the current record could not be found and so the
page won't be displayed. This error indicates that I've entered a bad value—to continue, I
press Esc to clear the dialog. (If you just click OK, Dreamweaver exits Live Data view.) Then
enter another value in the URL parameter field and press Enter (Return) to continue testing.

FORM-AL TESTING

Live Data view is good not only for
testing URL parameters, as discussed
in the previous tip, but also for
checking form-encoded values. As
I'm sure you remember from HTML
Forms 101, a form using the GET
method passes the values via the
URL parameter, whereas a POST
method form sends the info in the
body of the message sent to the
server. You've seen how the URL
parameter field works—to test

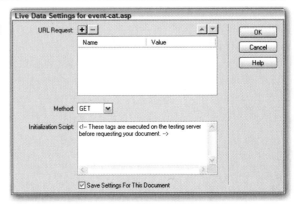

values for a POST form, select Live Data Settings from the Live Data toolbar and enter
the needed name/value pairs. The names will correspond to the form field names and the
values are what the user enters or selects. Be sure to change the Method to POST. This will
hide the unneeded URL parameter field; to get it back, change the Method to GET.

   YOU BE DE MASTER, I'LL BE DE TAIL

Master-detail pages are an essential type of web
application, usable in many different situations—
and Dreamweaver treats them with the respect
they deserve. You can either create a master-
detail page set by hand or use choose Insert >
Application Objects > Master Detail Page Set and
have Dreamweaver build it for you. The first way
gives you far more flexibility in terms of layout;
however, the second method is much faster.

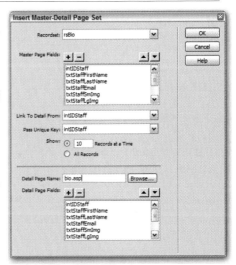

Here's one tip if you're working with
Dreamweaver objects. When creating the recordset for the master page, you might find it quicker
to keep the default All Columns option; this will
allow you to select any field you want to include
on either the master or the detail page—the
same recordset is copied to the detail page and
slightly modified. Then, after both pages have been created, return to the recordset on the
individual pages and reduce the fields, if necessary. By the way, the detail page needs to be
in the same folder as the master page for the code generated by the Master Detail Page Set
object to work.

SERVER BEHAVIOR BATTLE BOTS

Two of Dreamweaver's standard server behaviors don't get along very well. Go to Related Page and Move To Specific Record are not compatible and cannot be used together. Here's the problem: if you use Go To Related Page to link to a file which uses Move To Specific Record, the latter server behavior overwrites the URL values passed by the former. A better, more harmonious approach would be to avoid using the Move To Specific Record server behavior altogether. Instead, filter your recordset with the values passed from a URL parameter or form element.

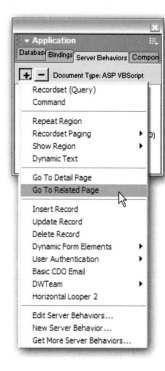

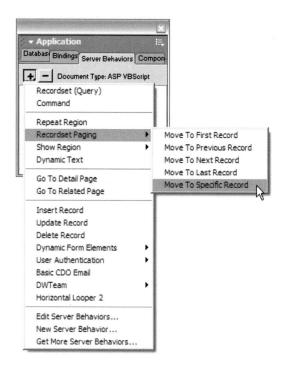

MAPPING FORM ELEMENTS AND DATA FIELDS

Both the Insert Record and Update Record server behaviors are essential to about half of the web application work I do, which is devoted to administrative chores. Although their use is greatly appreciated, they can be a bit of a chore to set up, especially if you have a lot of fields. You'll find that a great deal of time is spent mapping the form elements on the page to the fields in the data source. Careful planning can completely eliminate this time-intensive phase. If you name each form element with the same name as its corresponding database field,

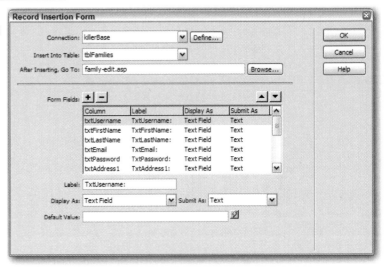

Dreamweaver will automatically map one to the other when applying either the Insert Record or Update Record server behavior. Moreover, you have a little flexibility because this feature is not case-sensitive. The first time you see Dreamweaver complete this task in seconds, you'll agree that it's a beautiful thing.

   MULTIPURPOSE CHECKBOXES, CHECK!

Dynamic checkboxes are a great visual way to display whether a Yes/No (a.k.a. Boolean) data field is true or false, right? If that's all you've been using them for, you're missing out on a cool application. When applying Dreamweaver's Dynamic

Check Box server behavior, you can set the checkbox to be selected if the data in a field is equal to any value, not just true or false. Let's say, for example, you have a web application that shows the status of a project. You could have a series of checkboxes in columns labeled Not Started, Halfway There, Almost Done, and Finished! Use the Dynamic Check Box server behavior to set the respective text values to 0%, 50%, 90% and 100% and you'll have a very visual representation of where each project stands.

HIDING THE PRIMARY KEYS

Here's a solution to a veritable hair-pulling problem. I was working on an update page and I had all the form fields neat and tidy on the page. I added the Update Record server behavior and started to work my way down the dialog. When it came time to specify the Unique Key

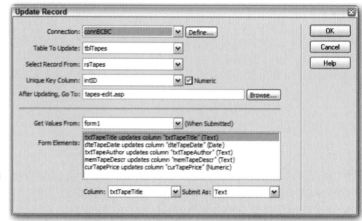

Column (also known as the primary key), I was stumped. Dreamweaver only displayed those fields that had been assigned to a form field element. The primary key for my table was, as usual, an auto-number field—and I certainly didn't want to make it possible for the user to change the auto-number, so the primary key wasn't available. The solution is hidden— hidden form field, that is. For Update Record situations, place a hidden form field on the page and, from the Bindings panel, drag the primary key field onto the hidden field. Open the Update Record server behavior and you'll find your primary key field available and ready for use. The same technique can be used for the Delete Record server behavior.

   TO LOCK OR UNLOCK: THAT IS THE QUESTION

Templates and dynamic applications are a real powerhouse combination. Many web applications are composed of similar, if not the same basic layout where only the dynamic content changes. In Dreamweaver MX, server-side code can be added to templates outside the `<html>` tags. This added functionality is really super because it means changes can be made easily to both the server and static page elements; you could, for example, add a Restrict Access to Page server behavior to a template and instantly protect a full slate of pages. Dreamweaver also offers another degree of control of which you may not be aware: the area outside the `<html>` tags can be locked or editable, just like a region on the page. By default, this external area is unlocked, which allows server-side code to be added to any documents derived from a template. To lock the region, add this code in the `<head>` area:

```
<!-- TemplateInfo codeOutsideHTMLIsLocked="true" -->
```

After saving your template and updating the associated pages, template instances will no longer be able to add or edit server-side code that is written outside the `<html>` tags.

I'D GO OFFLINE, IF ONLY I HAD THE CACHE

Don't always have a data source connection? Fear not! You can continue working, you lucky dog, as long as your cache is enabled. You probably didn't realize it, but to speed up development of web applications, Dreamweaver caches recordsets and other dynamic content, such as session variables and JavaBeans. This means that if you drop

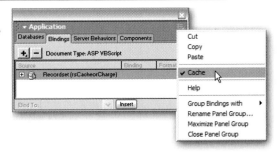

your data source connection for whatever reason, you can still apply the dynamic content to the page by dragging elements from the Bindings panel or inserting a server behavior. To make sure that the cache is up and running, choose the Options menu from the Bindings panel; by default, the Cache option is checked. Unfortunately, the cache is not all powerful—you won't be able to modify the existing recordsets, add new ones, or enter into Live Data view without an active data source connection. But then, you know what they say, "Cache isn't everything."

   ## SELECT ONE, SELECT 'EM ALL

When working with lists/menu form elements, you have an option to enable multiple selection. Well, I'll see your multiple select and raise you a "Select All." You can very easily add a list option that selects any entry—a very helpful feature when creating search pages. To create such an option, choose your list and then, from the Property inspector, choose Dynamic. In the Dynamic List/Menu dialog, add a new entry to the static list by select-

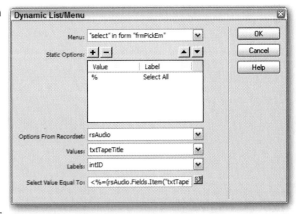

ing Add (+). Enter any desired label, such as Select All, and under the Value column enter a percent sign, %. The percent sign serves as a wildcard and makes any data value valid.

Pedal to the Metal

No Clicking Coding Zone

If you're not the hand-coding type or you think that you already know how to hand-code, you may think you can afford to skip this chapter. Don't even think

Pedal to the Metal
cool coding tricks

about it! In my observations of other developers, I've noticed that there are three kinds of hand-coders: There's the mouse-user extraordinaire who will do practically everything with the mouse and uses the keyboard as little as possible. There are the keyboard geniuses who avoid using the mouse at all costs. (I know one developer who looks like he's making love to his keyboard!) The rest who fall somewhere in-between—folks who quite possibly may not be working as efficiently as they could be because they don't know the ins and outs of doing things with the keyboard or the mouse.

That's what this chapter is all about— working with code efficiently—while either in Code or Design view. Yes, you can even hand-code while working in Design view. Anyone can hand-code—even the most horrible typists, go figure! Whether you're an experienced hand-coder, or a complete hand-coding virgin you're bound to pick up some super time-saving tips in this chapter. Don't be afraid to get your hands dirty in the code—after all, that's what a good antibacterial soap is for, right?

MOVING THINGS AROUND IN YOUR HEAD

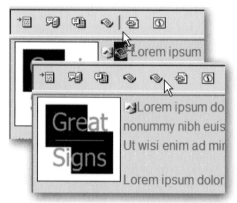

Several tags are stored in the `<head>` of an HTML document. Dreamweaver makes it easy for you to move the items already contained in the `<head>` to another position within the code. To toggle the head content area, select View > Head Content or Ctrl+Shift+W (Command+Shift+W). After it is visible, you'll see an icon that represents each of the tags located in the `<head>`. You can click and drag any of these icons to reorder its position within the code. There is one exception, however; the `<style>` tag cannot be moved with this method, although you can move surrounding head elements before or after the tag.

You also can drag various elements, such as comment tags or script tags, by their Invisible Elements marker directly into the head content area. If you want to get an element out of your head content, select its icon and then press the Delete key. I really like to use this feature when working with multiple CSS files so that I can see that they are listed in the correct order. You may find this helpful just for keeping your code in order in general.

   OOPS, BACKSPACE…

You're hand-coding, the code hint pops up, and you make a typo…so, of course, you instinctively press the Backspace key. The only problem is that now you don't get the code hints until you press the spacebar again. Instead of pressing the Backspace key once, you press it again, and then press the spacebar so you can move forward once and see the code hints again. Gee, what a pain that is! You needn't go through that anymore. Next time you make a mistake, press Backspace to remove your error, and then press Ctrl+spacebar (Command+spacebar) to pop up the code hints menu once again. Your cursor stays in place; it does not move forward. Now you can take advantage of the code hints provided.

This technique works in Code view or the Quick Tag Editor. If you've altered the timing of Code Hints in Preferences, this shortcut can also come in handy to display the hints faster than your Preferences setting.

OBSESSIVE-COMPULSIVE CODE FORMATTING

It's rather disgusting how important neat code has become to me. I don't know how I got this bad, but Dreamweaver makes it so easy to be so anal about code formatting that I just can't help myself. Commands > Apply Source Formatting snaps code into place based on the preferences set in Edit > Tag Libraries. Being the keyboard shortcut fanatic that I am, this menu option just wasn't enough for me. Select Edit > Keyboard Shortcuts and assign a keyboard shortcut to the Apply Source Formatting command. I happened to choose Ctrl+Shift+Backspace (Command+Shift+ Backspace) because it was free. If you're as finicky as I am, you'll even assign a similar shortcut, such as Ctrl+Backspace (Command+Backspace), to the Apply Source Formatting to Selection command.

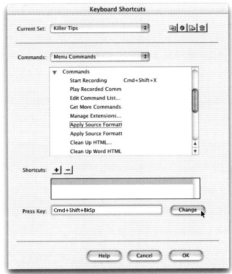

CLICK-N-DRAG OBJECTS

Some objects found in the Insert bar are available only in Design view. For this tip, most objects will work in either Code or Design view, just be sure to give either view focus before you try this. Did you know that you can click the objects in the Insert bar and then drag them into position within the Code or Design view? This may not sound useful at first because you could just position your cursor and click the object to insert it. If you're like me, you click the button, and then realize, "Oops, that's not where I want to put this." Too late now—you've got to Edit > Undo or Ctrl+Z (Command+Z) and try again. Instead of releasing that click, you could drag the object where you *do* want the object to be inserted.

  ● **WHAT A CHARACTER!**

I think it is fairly safe to say that most people don't memorize all the keyboard shortcuts for special characters. The Other Characters object and the Insert > Special Characters > Other menu call upon a dialog that offers 99 different special characters for you to choose from. It's almost like having the Windows Character map (or Key Caps on Macintosh) right inside Dreamweaver.

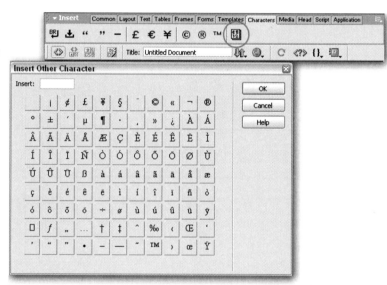

If 99 characters just aren't enough for you, there is a way to access roughly 255 instead as long as you have Code Hints enabled in Preferences.

If you can recognize the character itself or its named entity, you can hand-code it easily in Dreamweaver; you don't even need to know the keyboard shortcuts! In Code view, type an ampersand (**&**) and it will bring up the code hints for all "named" special characters (numbered special characters do not have code hints). Then press the next letter in the name until the special character you want is highlighted, and press Enter (Return). Alternatively, you can press the down-arrow key to highlight a named character and then press Enter (Return).

 COLOR YOURSELF HAPPY...

One of the things that changed dramatically in Dreamweaver MX is the way the program handles code coloring. Apparently, the new colors used in MX were an effort to make Dreamweaver MX use syntax coloring that matches other Macromedia products. That was a nice move on Macromedia's part, but they even took it a step further by allowing you to customize your code with your chosen colors.

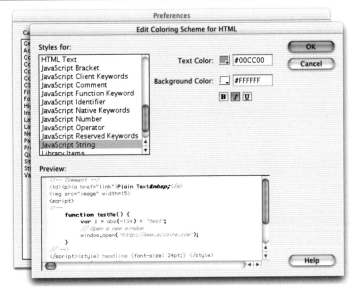

JavaScript strings is one syntax color change from Dreamweaver 4 to MX that I just had to get back. With plain text and JavaScript strings colored black, I can't tell at a glance whether I've made proper use of quotation marks. If the strings are colored green (#00CC00), I can see immediately that I've made a mistake when I notice that the code turns black.

To access Code Coloring options, choose Edit > Preferences (Dreamweaver > Preferences on Mac OS X) or Ctrl+U (Command+U) and then select Code Coloring from the list that appears on the left. In the Document type list, select HTML and then click Edit Coloring Scheme. This is so cool; you don't even need to know the official name for the syntax you want to customize. Just click (in the Preview area) the type of code you want to change and the formatting options will change to match. In our case, scroll down in the Preview area and click the Allaire URL, http://www.allaire.com. JavaScript String is now selected in the Styles for list. (Yes, you could have just selected JavaScript String in the list above, but I think it is more fun to use the Preview area.) Now that JavaScript String is selected, choose a text color using the color swatch's color picker or type a hexadecimal value (#00CC00). If you'd like, you can even set a background color and bold, italics, or underlined formatting. After you've made your choices, you'll see that the Allaire URL is now colored.

Keep in mind that you've set this only for HTML documents. You'll need to make the change for each document type in which you intend to use JavaScript. Chances are that you'll want to do this for the JavaScript document type and your server model of choice at the very least. As you can see, code coloring is not limited to JavaScript; the list of options is quite extensive.

ANYBODY SEEN MY CODE?

I was originally introduced to snippets when Massimo Foti created his Classic Snippets Panel for Dreamweaver 4. Now Dreamweaver MX users have similar functionality built right in with the Snippets panel. Next time you find yourself hunting down a piece of code, add it to your snippets arsenal. Whenever you need that code, you'll know it is in the Snippets panel and available for quick, easy insertion into your document. Even though the Snippets panel comes with hundreds

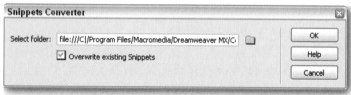

of sample snippets, the most valuable ones are those you create and are able to reuse repeatedly.

Snippets are not site-specific; they're available to you for use in any site definition. One thing to keep in mind is that snippets created in HomeSite, ColdFusion Studio, JRun Studio, or Massimo Foti's Classic Snippets panel are not the same file format as those in Dreamweaver MX. There is a handy extension by Massimo Foti, the Snippets Converter, that you can use to convert those programs' format of snippets into Dreamweaver MX's format. The converter is available at http://www.dwfaq.com/Snippets/converter.asp. You can find hundreds of useful snippets at the Snippets Exchange http://www.dwfaq.com/Snippets/.

PUTTING A DENT IN THE CODE, OR TAKING THEM OUT

Neatly formatted code is far easier to read and troubleshoot than messy code. Part of what makes code neat is the care that developers take when indenting lines. If Commands > Apply Source Formatting doesn't quite get it right, you do have the option to do additional formatting manually. I find these shortcuts most helpful when hand-coding JavaScript or server-side code. There is a better combo of keyboard shortcuts than the old Tab or Shift+Tab combo, which doesn't require any selection at all to indent or outdent entire lines of code. Try using Ctrl+Shift+> (Command+Shift+>) to indent the line(s) or Ctrl+Shift+< to outdent the line(s). To help you remember which shortcut is which, the angle is pointing to the direction the code will be moved.

MAKING SELECTIONS EFFECTIVELY

Let's look at the two extreme types of coders—keyboard geniuses, and mouse-users extraordinaire—and find out how they do the same actions.

The keyboard genius:

- Selects a single character, holding the Shift key while pressing either the left- or the right-arrow key.
- Selects an entire word or set of contiguous characters, using Ctrl+Shift while maneuvering the cursor with the left- or the right-arrow key. This action will treat characters other than underscores and alphanumeric characters as a separate selection, despite their being in a set of contiguous characters, and includes spaces or line returns at the end of the selection. The single character selection method may be used to move the cursor more precisely.
- Uses the Shift+down- or up-arrow keys to select or deselect an entire line of code.

The mouse-user extraordinaire:

- Clicks and drags to select a single character, or for multiple characters, Shift+clicks once at the start of the selection and again at the end.
- Double-clicks within the string of characters for a single word or set of contiguous characters. This method includes alphanumeric characters and underscores in selections and treats all other characters as separate selections. The benefit to using this method is that it does not include spaces as part of the selection and includes line returns only if you've clicked at the end of a line.
- Clicks the line number to select a single line of code, and then hold the Shift key and clicks again on the line number where you want your selection to end.

The important thing isn't to become either a mouse or keyboard fanatic, but to know which options work best for the situation you're in so that you can use them as needed and improve your workflow.

GIMME A HINT, PLEASE

Code hints and tag completion make hand-coding for a typlexic person like me so much easier. (See http://www.typlexia.com for more info.) So if you thought you were doomed to Design view due to lack of typing skills, you're in for a treat.

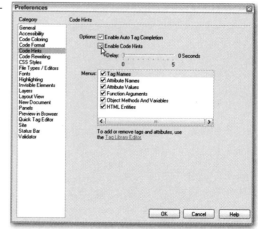

If you've never customized the Code Hints category of Preferences before, tag completion and code hints will be already enabled. Tag completion means that after you type the closing angle bracket of the opening tag, the closing tag will be added automatically for you.

Following the opening `<body>` tag, let's start coding a table. Begin by typing the opening angle bracket, and then type **t**. As soon as you press the key, table is highlighted in the list. Go ahead and press Enter (Return). Now, type a space, and a list of available attributes for the `<table>` tag will appear. Let's add a background color; type **bg** and that highlights the bgcolor attribute we want, so press Enter (Return). Check it out; the color picker appeared! Use your arrow keys to maneuver to the color you want to use and then press Enter (Return) or use the mouse to select one. After you select or type the color value, your cursor automatically moves past the bgcolor attribute's closing quotation mark. When you are adding an attribute that doesn't offer a hint for the value, you'll need to use your right-arrow key to move past the closing quotation mark.

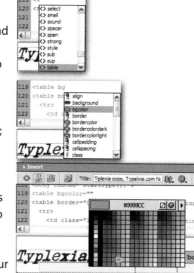

INSERT HTML

You're working in Design view—yes even "real" hand-coders do that sometimes—and you realize that you need to insert an HTML tag, what should you do? You could switch to Code view and do it there, use the Tag Chooser object, or hand-code it from Design view.

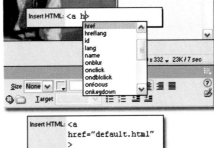

Truth be told, all of the options will work—and there are actually a few others you'll read about later in this chapter—but the Quick Tag Editor can help you add that tag quickly and easily.

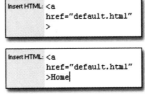

To access the Quick Tag Editor, you could click the pencil icon in the upper-right corner of the Property inspector; choose Insert HTML from the document's context menu; select Quick Tag Editor from the Modify menu; or use the Ctrl+T (Command+T) keyboard shortcut.

`<a href="default.html">Home</a>`

When the Quick Tag Editor appears, type the tag and any attributes then, without typing the closing tag, press Enter (Return) to return to the document and close the Quick Tag Editor. Dreamweaver adds the closing tag for you. Your cursor is automatically placed between the opening and closing of the tag you just entered. That's what I call convenient.

   REFRESH DESIGN VIEW

While you are working simultaneously in Code and Design views, you will notice that Design view does not update as you make edits in Code view—and with good reason. Imagine how annoying it would be for Design view to keep updating itself. Another reason for this is that Design view may take some time to refresh, which would slow you down while hand-coding. If you need to see the changes you make in Code view in Design view, press the F5 keyboard shortcut for Refresh Design View or select the command from the View menu. As you might expect, clicking in Design view will update the Document window.

QUICK TAG EDITING

You already learned how to insert HTML quickly, but you could also use the Quick Tag Editor to—you guessed it—edit HTML tags. In fact, the Quick Tag Editor can be used for XML too. In Design view, place your cursor in the element you need to modify. Then right-click (Ctrl+click) a tag in the Tag Selector and then choose Edit Tag from the context menu that appears.

The Quick Tag Editor should now be open with the phrase Edit Tag shown above the tag to indicate the mode you're viewing. Now you can edit the tag to your heart's content without having to go to Code view.

   WRAP TAG MODE

Every now and then, there will come a time when you'll need to wrap a selection with a specific HTML tag. Superscript and subscript are perfect examples of cases in which you might want to use this technique. Let's say that you want to make a trademark symbol superscript. First, add the trademark symbol (you'll find it in the Characters category of the Insert bar), and then make sure that you have it selected in

Design view. Now press Ctrl+T (Command+T) and the Quick Tag Editor appears in Wrap Tag mode. (If the Quick Tag Editor appears in a different mode, press the keyboard shortcut again until it displays that it is in Wrap Tag mode.) Now all you need to do is type **sup** and press Enter (Return). You'll see the trademark symbol elevated as superscript text. In the same way, you can create subscript text (for example, H_2O). Instead of typing, **sup**, this time you'll type **sub**. The selected text is wrapped with the $<sup>$ or $<sub>$ tag pairs, respectively.

Dreamweaver MX
KillerTips

PSYCHIC HELP

Few people can actually memorize every tag and its respective attributes. Go ahead and try this:

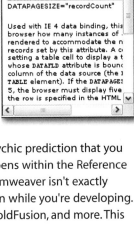

(1) Insert a table using whichever method you prefer.

(2) Click inside the opening `<table>` tag, and then press the spacebar to display code hints.

(3) Select datashapesize from the list, and give the attribute a value of 3. Do you know what the datapagesize attribute does? It isn't very common, so it is unlikely that you do. That's okay; read on…

Now that you've added this attribute, you are probably curious what its purpose is within the `<table>` tag. Click the attribute or highlight it, and then press Shift+F1. Dreamweaver makes a psychic prediction that you want to know about this attribute. The O'Reilly HTML reference opens within the Reference panel to the `<table>` tag's datapagesize description. OK, so Dreamweaver isn't exactly psychic; more like context-sensitive. Still, this is a great way to learn while you're developing. You can refer to the Reference panel for info on HTML, CSS, ASP, ColdFusion, and more. This sure beats digging through books to find the info you need!

ATTRIBUTE ADDING MADE EASY

Often the Property inspector doesn't contain enough fields for all the attributes of the current tag; that's when you turn to the Tag inspector. The upper portion of the Tag inspector is a tree view of the current document's structure. The bottom portion displays a property sheet of possible attributes for the current tag. What's great about this is that you can use the Tab key to go from attribute to attribute, filling in values for only the ones you need. If you need an attribute that isn't listed, you can enter it manually at the end of the property sheet. What's even greater about the Tag inspector as a whole is that it also works with XML documents.

If the attribute value should or could be of a certain type, extra icons appear to the right of the value's field. You'll find the lightning bolt icon available for many of the listed attributes because you could potentially pull a record as a value. Other icons include the color button for choosing colors and the point-to-file and folder icon for attributes whose value requires a path to a file. The same code hints that are available to you while hand-coding are listed in the drop-down list; however, you must click the drop-down list's down arrow and select the item from the list.

TAG CHOOSER

The Tag chooser is the last icon in the Common category of the Insert bar. If you wanted to, you could actually build the entire structure of your document from this single object. Tags are categorized on the left of the Tag Chooser dialog. If a folder is selected, all tags are displayed on the right; if a subcategory is selected, a more specific list of tags appears there. All you have to do is choose a tag and click Insert.

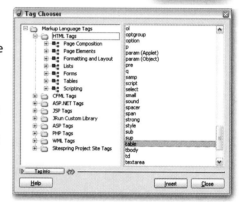

If there is a Tag Editor dialog available for the chosen tag, it will be displayed next; otherwise, the Tag Chooser dialog retains focus. You can keep adding tags to your heart's content—just be sure your cursor is positioned where you want the tag to be inserted. If you need to know more about the currently selected tag, click the Tag Info button to expand the dialog to display reference material if available or use the Reference panel icon instead. When you're finished adding tags, click Close. It's just that easy.

   WRAPPING CODE LINES

Chances are that you don't want to be bothered with scrolling to the right to see an entire line of code—at least I know I don't! So what I have done is enabled the Word Wrap from View Options icon on the Document toolbar

and/or the Code inspector's View Options icon. Selecting View > Code View Options > Word Wrap controls only Code view and not the Code inspector; you'll need to use the View Options method for the Code inspector. Lines of code in excess of the Code window's width will wrap to the next line. To help you distinguish what is actually a new line and what is a wrapped line, be sure that Line Numbers is also checked in the View Options icon's menu.

DO NOT PASS GO, GO DIRETLY TO LINE NUMBER

We've all had pages that contain a JavaScript error at some point. When the browser tells us that we have an error on a specific line number, we're anxious to look at that line to see what is causing the trouble. Don't bother scrolling to get there, just

use the Go to Line Number command, which is available only when Code view or when the Code inspector has focus. Select Edit > Go to Line or use the Ctrl+G (Command+G) keyboard shortcut. When the Go to Line Number dialog appears, type the line number and press Enter (Return) or click OK. The document scrolls (if necessary) and your cursor is placed at the start of the specified line number. The Go to Line command is especially handy when you're working in long documents with hundreds of lines of code.

   ## WHERE'S THAT FUNCTION?

JavaScript files can get mighty complicated and lengthy. Keeping track of where you put which function so that you can go back to it easily requires an excellent memory—or Dreamweaver's assistance. Located in the Document toolbar is the Code Navigation icon (that's the one that looks like a pair of curly braces and is enabled only while editing code). When clicked, the Code Navigation icon displays a drop-down list containing the names of all the functions in the current document. The functions listed may be either JavaScript or VBScript and are in the order in which they appear on the page. If you'd like the functions to appear in alphabetical order, you can Ctrl+click (Command+click) the Code Navigation icon. Clicking any of the functions listed will select its name and take you to it. Now you're in the code exactly where you want to be; exceptionally convenient!

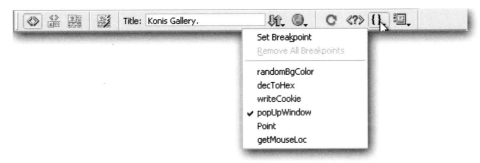

PUTTING YOUR HEADS TOGETHER

Do you remember learning how to move things around in your `<head>` earlier in this chapter? Now you're going to learn how to put your `<head>`s together. Here's the scenario: You have one document that has some `<meta>` tags that you need in a second document. You can go directly to the code and copy and paste what you need, but there is a simpler way that even works while you are in Design view (remember that you can hand-code in Design view, too).

First select View > Head Content or press Ctrl+Shift+W (Command+Shift+W) to enable the Head Content bar if it is not already visible (in both documents you're working with). Now click the icon of the `<meta>` tag you want to copy to the other document. Select Edit > Copy or press Ctrl+C (Command+C). Switch to the second document and click anywhere on the Head Content bar that is not occupied by another icon and then paste using either Edit > Paste or Ctrl+V (Command+V). Dreamweaver places the `<meta>` tag just before the closing `</head>` tag and its icon will appear last in the Head Content bar. Oh, you'd rather it appear where you want it in the first place? Okay, no problem—you can do that. Don't click an empty area of the Head Content; instead, click an icon and when you paste, the code will be added to the code just after your selected icon.

CHANGING TAGS

Every now and then there comes a time when you need to change a tag to an entirely different tag. One quick and easy way to do this is in the Tree menu of the Tag inspector. Right-click (Ctrl+click) a tag in the Tag inspector's tree menu, select the Options menu and choose Edit, or double-click the tag to make it editable. The entire tag should be selected, so just press the Backspace key to remove the entire tag if you like, or just type over it. Type the tag

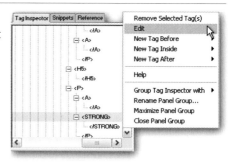

with or without the angle brackets; Dreamweaver will add the angle brackets if you leave them off. Now press Enter (Return) and you'll see that the tag has been replaced in both the document tree and the actual code. If appropriate, Dreamweaver even changes the closing tag.

BACK AND FORTH

This is probably the quickest way to get to exactly where you need to be in the code to do your editing and get back to Design view when done. Instead of scrolling through Code view to get where you need to be, first click in Design view and then press Ctrl+Backquote (Command+Backquote) to switch to the area of Code view that corresponds to the cursor's position in Design view. (Never heard of Backquote before? It's the same as the Tilde [~] key.) Use the same shortcut to jump to the place in Design view that corresponds to Code view. If you're the menu-using type, you could use View > Switch Views to toggle back and forth between Code and Design views. If you're using Code and Design views simultaneously, your cursor position is all that changes, but if you're using one view or another, the actual view changes and places your cursor accordingly.

   DO YOU VALIDATE?

Whenever I pay for parking, I ask the business I'm visiting whether they validate parking. This can save you quite a bit in parking fees if they do. Consider that a bonus tip to the one I'm about to share with you. It has become increasingly important to write good clean code for browsers to represent the documents in the expected manner. For the most part, Dreamweaver does an excellent job of keeping your code valid and properly written; however, Dreamweaver can only do so much itself. The rest is up to us to tell Dreamweaver what we want done or hand-code it ourselves.

In the Validation panel, Dreamweaver can check your document against various validation specs and list warnings and errors for you. Select File > Check Page > Validate Markup or use the keyboard shortcut Shift+F6 to begin the process. A list of errors and warnings appears in the Validation panel of which you can double-click to jump to that line number in the code—even if you're in Design view, Code view opens so that both views are visible. If you're not sure what any of the listed items mean from their descriptions alone, select the entry and then use the Options menu or right-click (Ctrl+click) to select More Info. You also can use the context menu or Options menu to choose Settings, where you can pick and choose which types of validation checking should be done.

 NOTE TO SELF...

Dreamweaver's Design Notes feature is touted as a tool for communicating in a team of developers. You don't have to use it that way, though! Instead of making a backup copy of a file and cluttering a site with multiple versions of a file, create a Design Note instead. It is always a good idea to backup your site before making edits, but this quick-and-dirty method is suitable in many cases. One word of caution, if Design Notes are uploaded to the server, they are publicly accessible; do not put any private info into a Design Note.

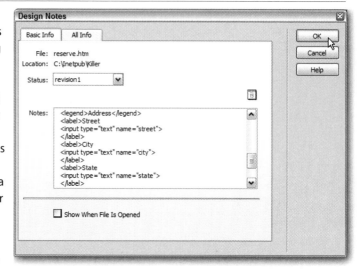

To add a Design Note, right-click (Ctrl+click) the file in the Site panel and select Design Notes from the context menu or double-click in the Notes column to the right of the file with which you want the Design Note to be associated. Paste the

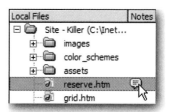

code into the text area and check the box if you'd like the Design Note to appear each time the file is opened. Click OK when you are done. Unless you've disabled Design Notes in your site definition, you should see an icon in the Notes column of the expanded Site panel. Double-click that icon anytime you need to view the note. Now you know exactly where to look for information about that particular file. By the way, Design Notes work on all file types listed in your Site panel. Feel free to add any type of notation you need, be it reminders, file status, backup code, or anything else you can imagine.

BOLD VERSUS STRONG, ITALICS VERSUS EMPHASIS

By now you may have noticed that anytime you use the Bold or Italics icons on the Property inspector, they don't insert `<b>` or `<i>` tags, respectively. Instead, for bold you get a `<strong>` tag pair and for italics you get an `<em>` tag pair. The reason for this is that `<strong>` and `<em>` actually add physical meaning to the text; voice-enabled browsers will read these words with a different tone. Whereas `<b>` and `<i>` do not add anything but visual meaning, which is of no help at all to those who rely on screen readers. Typically `<strong>` is displayed as bold and `<em>` is styled as italicized text, but you can ensure this with CSS and be certain that your text is as accessible as can be.

If you absolutely must have bold or italics though I don't recommend it, you can change your Preferences in the General category by disabling the last checkbox under Editing Options so that `<strong>` and `<em>` are not used in place of `<b>` and `<i>` when you are using the Property inspector. You'll still have the option of using `<strong>` and `<em>` from the Text category of the Insert bar.

▼ Insert	Common	Layout	Text	Tables	Frames	Forms	Templates	Characters	Media	Head	Script	Application

A₂ B I S em ¶ [""] PRE h1 h2 h3 ul ol li dl dt dd abbr. W3C

     CREATE YOUR OWN CODE HINTS

If you're creating XML documents or making custom ColdFusion or ASP.Net tags, you'll find the custom code hints feature especially useful. Edit > Tag Libraries not only lets you add custom tags, attributes, and their values; it also gives you complete control over the format of your code (see the next tip).

Using the Tag Library Editor is rather straightforward. Click the Add(+) button, select New Tags, and then choose the Tag Library folder you would like to add a tag to from the drop-down list. Now type the tag name, check the box if it should have a closing tag, and then click OK. The tag is represented by a folder within the Tag Library you chose. If the new tag has potential attributes or you'd like to add attributes to an existing tag, click the Add(+) button again, and choose New Attributes. Now select the Tag Library and the tag from the respective drop-down list, then type the attribute and click OK. Did you notice that the menu says tags and attributes, both plural? Try entering multiple tags or attributes separated by a comma. You can add as many tags or attributes at once as you like.

It gets even better; you can even add the type of values the attribute should suggest. Locate the tag in the tree menu and find the attribute you want to assign a type of value. After you've selected the attribute, you'll see an option to set the case of the attribute and a preview, but we're interested in the Attribute Type field. Most of your options should make sense to you, but I encourage you to make a fake tag with attributes of various types so that you know what to expect. The one that may not make sense right away is Enumerated. This is the only option that will enable the Values field where you can type a comma-separated list of possible attribute values. These values appear in a drop-down list when you're hand-coding the value, just like the align attribute pops up a list of center, justify, left, or right.

   COMPLETE FORMATTING CONTROL

Because you're now familiar with the Tag Library Editor from the previous tip, I thought you might want to know just a little bit more about what you can do with it. The default source formatting can sometimes yield undesirable results. Before Dreamweaver MX, you had to manually edit a certain file to get any sort of custom formatting—with quite a bit of trial and error. Now all it takes is selecting the tag in the Tag Library Editor, and then selecting Line Breaks, Contents and Case settings. Just remem-

ber that a tag's formatting depends not only on its own settings but the setting of Contents for the parent element containing the tag. You even get to see an example of how the code will look in the Preview field.

Customizing our Hot Rod

Your
Way

I never got into souping up or detailing cars when I was growing up—and, considering that my first car was a Pacer, that's probably a good thing. Perhaps that explains why

Customizing Your Hot Rod

customization and extensibility tips

I'm so crazy about the options in Dreamweaver for customization and extensibility. This stuff just (pick one)…(a) rocks my world, (b) floats my boat, or (c) christens my cabbage. (Sorry about that last one; I'm trying to start a new cliché and this one obviously needs some work.)

In this chapter, we've tried to collect for you the best tips from the realm that takes Dreamweaver to the next level. Consequently, you'll find tips for folks just starting out with customization by creating commands via the History panel (right next to the strategies for building floating panels). You'll also find some cool methods for customizing Dreamweaver that could actually make you some cash. Show you the money, you say? Just consider this chapter to be all over the map—and customizing and extending Dreamweaver takes a pretty big map—and use it as your guide to buried treasure.

Before you continue, read this quick note from our lawyers: Be forewarned that the investigation and usage of Macromedia Dreamweaver extensionology and customizabilitization is extremely addictive and could cause loss of sleep and momentary bouts of frustration coupled with vast stretches of oh-my-gosh-I-can't-believe-it-actually-works!-itis. Proceed at your own risk. Eat your vegetables. Christen the Cabbage.

Go forth and extend.

STRUCTURING HISTORY PANEL CREATED COMMANDS

Don't you just hate to do the same task over and over again? I do, and that's why I'm a History panel fanatic. Not only does the History panel (Window > Others > History panel) give a clear picture of almost every step you take in Dreamweaver, but you can easily transform those steps into a repeatable command. Years of building macros in Word taught me one basic rule to automating changes: end where you want to begin. Let's say that you have a standard list of names you want to put in lastname-comma-firstname order. All you need do in Dreamweaver is perform the operation on the first name—using only your keyboard, because the History panel doesn't record mouse clicks—and end by positioning the cursor so that it's ready to do the second line. In this case, here's what I would do:

(1) Place your cursor in front of the first name.

(2) Shift+select the first name.

(3) Cut it.

(4) Move to the end of the last name.

(5) Type a comma and a space.

(6) Paste the first name.

(7) Move your cursor in front of the next first name.

At this point, either select the steps in the History panel and click Replay or—if you see a continuing use for this operation—choose Save As Command. Either way, you're good to go, again and again and again.

COMMANDING THE TABLE

As the previous tip demonstrated, the History panel is great for making simple commands—but it has one big drawback: it won't record mouse movements. To get the most out of this Dreamweaver feature, you'll need to master your keyboard movement controls; for example, pressing Ctrl+right arrow (Command+right arrow) to move a word to the right. Movement within a table is generally controlled by its own set of keyboard shortcuts, such as pressing Tab to move forward or backward through the cells—unfortunately, Dreamweaver MX does not record tab movements. The best way to navigate within the cell, for History panel purposes, is with the arrow keys. Press the up arrow or down arrow to move the cursor to the beginning or end of the cell contents, respectively. If the cursor is at the end of the content, press right arrow to move to the first position of the next cell. Likewise, when the cursor is up front of a cell's content, pressing left arrow moves the cursor to the end of the previous cell.

   ## ALIAS: THE DREAMWEAVER COMMAND

Look out XHTML, there's a new sheriff in town and you'd better clean up your act. An old Dreamweaver workhorse command, Clean Up HTML, has been enhanced to also handle XHTML pages. Found under the Commands menu, this handy feature obligingly changes its name according to the page

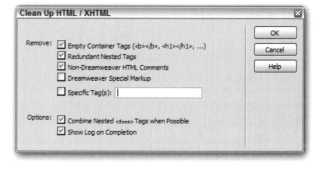

type: when a regular HTML page is the current one, you'll see Clean Up HTML in the menu; XHTML page users will see Clean Up XHTML. No matter what it's called, this command is great to run first when you get a page handed off to you and then again in the final stages of page design. With Clean Up HTML / XHTML, you can rid your page of unused tag pairs (like <h2> . . .</h2>) and redundant nested tags. The command also can strip out HTML comments whether they are the standard variety or Dreamweaver-specific comments. Be careful if you decide to go the latter route, however; removing Dreamweaver-inserted comments will also remove any template or library item functionality. One last tip for the Clean Up HTML / XHTML command: if you want to remove specific tags, just enter the text of the tag and not the full tag (for example, enter **b** for the bold tag instead of **<b>**). For multiple tags, enter them in a space separated list, like b i u.

   SOUND APPROACHES TO EDITING

Wherever possible, I really like including sound on a website. Although audio is not right for every site, when used judiciously sound adds an extra dimension to the user experience. Okay, okay, it's just cool. One of my favorite little tools for adjusting sound bites is QuickTime Pro. With it, you can resample sound files, convert from stereo to monophonic, crop a clip, and output to a wide range of formats. Nice, you say, but what does this have to do with Dreamweaver? I set Dreamweaver up to use

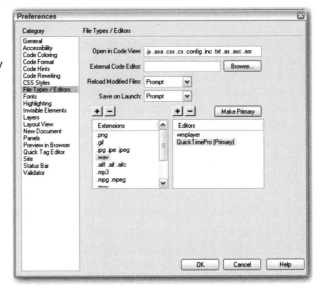

QuickTime Pro as the editor for .wav, .aiff, and other audio formats through the File Types/Editors category of Preferences. After I've established the editor preference, if it looks like a sound file is too big, I can just double-click the file from the Site panel to open it in QuickTime Pro for a quick trim or resample. When completed, I export the modified file and replace the existing file in my Dreamweaver site (knowing full well that my source file is safely tucked away). This approach also can be applied to any file you might include in Dreamweaver that is best edited by an external program.

A PLUS IN YOUR COLUMN

Websites being developed by teams have special challenges, such as being able to quickly see which pages are already done and which still need work. Dreamweaver's Site panel has customizable columns that can help keep everyone on the team clued in. To add a custom column, start in the Site panel. Windows users should then choose View > File View Columns, and Mac users should select Site > Site Files View > File View Columns from the main menu. After you have the File View Columns category of the Site Definitions dialog on the screen, choose Add (+) to insert a custom column. Give your new column a name in the Column

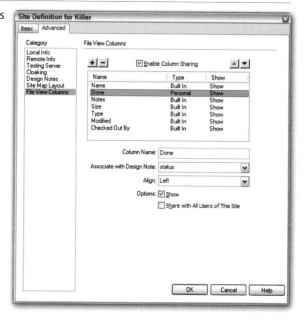

Name field and add a design note in the Associate with Design Note field. Change the alignment if you don't want to use the default Left position and make sure that the Show option is selected. When you return to the Site panel, you'll see that your new column is added for all files. To enter a column value for a file, click twice slowly in the column—a regular double-click opens the file. For a column showing the page's completion status, I prefer to use decimal numbers rather than words; I find that .10, .50 and .75 are properly sorted and more accurately tell the status rather than "almost done" or "nearly finished." So, with this system, how is a completed page labeled? Why, any developers worth their salt know that when it's done, it's 1.0.

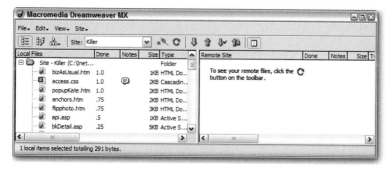

   THE MOTHER OF ALL MENUS

All of the menus found in Dreamweaver—including the main menu, all the panel menus, and the context menus—are controlled by a single XML file. Found in the Configuration/Menus folder, the menus.xml file is truly a mother lode of information and power. Want to know how Dreamweaver really executes a command? Check out the command's menu entry in menus.xml to see the file used or actual code executed. You can open and examine the file in Dreamweaver; if you plan on modifying it, however, be sure to open the version found in the Dreamweaver MX user's folder. You should also be sure to make a backup just in case of trouble; and if you really get in trouble, there is a Macromedia created backup in the same folder called menus.bak that will get you back on the right footing. After you've opened the file, you'll notice that all the shortcut definitions are at the top of the file. In my experience, these are best modified using the Keyboard Shortcut Editor found under the Edit menu. The fastest way to get to the main menu definitions is to search for "Main Window" (with or without the quotation marks) using Dreamweaver's Find and Replace feature. Happy Menu Spelunking!

```
1655  <menubar name="Main Window" id="DWMainWindow">
1656      <menu name="Apple" id="DWMenu_Apple" platform="mac">
1657          <menuitem name="About Macromedia Dreamweaver MX"           command="dw.showAboutBox()"
1658      </menu>
1659      <menu name="_File" id="DWMenu_File">
1660          <menuitem name="_New..."                    key="Cmd+N"        domRequired="false" ena
1661          <menuitem name="_Open..."            key="Cmd+O"        domRequired="false" enabled
1662          <menuitem name="Open in Fra_me..."   key="Cmd+Shift+O"  enabled="dw.canOpenInFrame(
1663          <menuitem name="_Close"              key="Cmd+W"        enabled="dw.getDocumentDOM(
1664          <menuitem name="_Close"              key="Cmd+W"        enabled="dw.getFocus() != '
1665          <separator />
```

WHAT ELSE IS ON THE MENU?

Following up on the previous tip, there are a few things you should know about the format of the menus.xml file. First, every main item (there are 10 in the standard Dreamweaver menu: File, Edit, View, etc.) contains a list of separate menu items. Each menu item contains a unique ID attribute and an optional keyboard shortcut. Whether the menu item is displayed is controlled by the enabled attribute; if the enabled attribute evaluates as true, the item is available; if it's false, the menu item is disabled. What determines the function of a menu item? There are two possible, mutually exclusive attributes: command and file. The command attribute takes a JavaScript function, often a Dreamweaver API call; for example, the command value for the File > Save All menu item is dw.saveAll(). The second attribute, file, points to a HTML file in the Configuration folder which contains JavaScript too complex to fit in a single line or opens a dialog box. When you are modifying the menus.xml file, you need to take extreme care to properly code your entries. Dreamweaver disables the menu items containing any entries with incorrect syntax. For complete details, see Help > Extending Dreamweaver.

LET'S ALL PLAY THIRD-PARTY TAG!

Look up any good reference of HTML and you're going to get a standard set of tags. But, because HTML is so flexible—and browsers are so tolerant of tags they don't understand—extension developers often employ a healthy dose of non-HTML or third-party tags. When might a third-party tag be used? Here's one example: I co-developed a Dreamweaver extension called Deva which builds navigation systems, like table of contents and indexes. With Deva, any text can be marked as an index item which surrounds the text with a `<index>...</index>` tag pair. The `<index>` tag is a Deva third-party tag and, as such, highlights the enclosed text. The highlight allows the designer to quickly identify specially marked passages. Third-party tags are defined by enclosing an XML file in the Configuration/ThirdPartyTags folder. Here's the entry for the Deva `<index>` tag:

```
<tagspec tag_name="index" tag_type="nonempty" render_contents="true"
content_model="marker_model"></tagspec>
```

In addition to their highlight capability, third-party tags can also be represented by icons—in which case the `render_contents` attribute would be `false` and a .gif image, also stored in the ThirdPartyTags folder, is named.

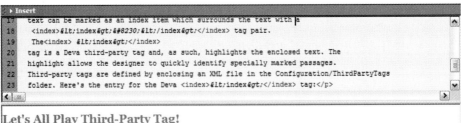

FREE SCRIPTS, GET YOUR FREE SCRIPTS RIGHT HERE!

Pssssttt! Want a great collection of JavaScript functions and utilities guaranteed to ramp up your extensibility productivity? I can let you have it for a song…and that song is "Dreamweaver," of course. Included with every installation of Dreamweaver is a terrific number of JavaScript files containing a key functionality for almost every operation an extension developer needs. Why is it so extensive? Simple—because these scripts are the same ones used by the Macromedia engineers to give Dreamweaver its power. You'll find the scripts in the Dreamweaver MX/Configuration/Shared folder in a couple of places. The older but still useful scripts are found in the Shared/MM/Scripts folder; the newer ones are in the Shared/Common/

Scripts folder. There are too many scripts and functions to describe here, but one of my favorites is enableControl.js, found in the Shared/MM/Scripts/CMN folder. In Dreamweaver, this function is used by the Master Detail Page Set application object, among others. Once you include this file, you're programatically able to enable or disable a dialog's form controls by calling one function. It's the essence of *schweet*.

EMO, THE EXTENSION MANAGER

What, you mean you don't name your utilities? The Extension Manager is a key component in Macromedia's strategy for the MX line. One of the obvious bottom-line benefits of Dreamweaver, Fireworks, and Flash is their extensibility.

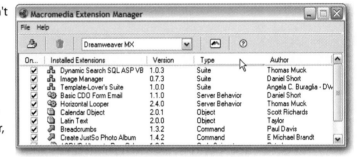

To really take advantage of the extensions being produced for the programs, a central storage facility, the Macromedia Exchange, was developed—along with a central tool for managing them: the Extension Manager.

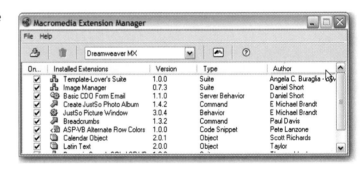

The Extension Manager is accessible from a couple of places—under both the Commands and Help menu as Manage Extensions.

After you've installed a number of extensions, you are ready to take advantage of the Extension Manager's special features. If you have a lot of extensions, you can quickly find the one you are looking for by using the sorting capabilities of each column. In addition to sorting by name, you also can sort by extension author and type. Very handy when you're trying to track down a behavior and can't remember which one it is. Another useful feature is the On/Off toggle. To disable an installed extension, just uncheck its entry. Why not just uninstall, you say? Sometimes you want to disable an extension only temporarily—often because of conflicts with another extension—and the On/Off toggle is far more efficient than uninstalling and reinstalling.

   COLOR ME EXTENSIBLE

If you've looked at all into creating your own Dreamweaver extensions, you may be aware that the user interface for them is based on HTML forms. This counts as an entry in both the plus and the minus columns; it's an advantage because that makes it easy to build interfaces right in Dreamweaver, and it's a disadvantage because HTML form elements are pretty limited in functionality. The Dreamweaver engineers have heard the cries of woe of extension authors everywhere and responded with a some nifty additional controls. Top of my list is the color picker. The color picker is used throughout the Dreamweaver interface. Whenever the

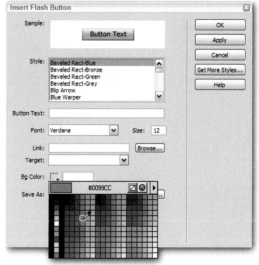

user needs to choose a color, that little box pops open a whole palette of colors, complete with an eyedropper for sampling. You can add a color picker to your extension by dropping code like this in your HTML form:

```
<input type="mmcolorbutton" name="myColorPicker" value="">
```

You need to specify an `<input>` tag with a `type` attribute of `mmcolorbutton` and a unique name. The value attribute is optional; without it, the user sees the default gray color. You are, of course, free to specify a value to preset the color, if you like. Make mine puce, please.

EDITABLE AND SELECTABLE? INCREDIBLE!

Speaking of cool input controls (as we were in the previous tip), here's one that I've long lusted for. Many of the drop-down lists used on standard program user interfaces (not web applications), allow the user to type in their own value

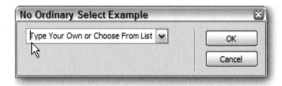

if they don't see something they like in the list. (Remember "Everybody, Come On and Do Da Combo, Mon!" in Chapter 7?) In the trade, this is known as an *editable select list*. To convert a `<select>` list in Dreamweaver to editable format takes years of training and several man-years of labor. Or, you could just add these attributes to the tag: `editable="true" edittext="some default value"`. You must use the edittext attribute, but you can leave the value empty. That's it. Now all the items on the list are editable. Often, a user interface design might call for the first item in the list to be blank, indicating that it's editable. In such cases, the select tag would look like this:

```
<select name="mainList" editable="true" edittext="">
```

As with standard `<select>` lists, the `selectedIndex` property is used to determine which item the user chose. If an editable list item was selected, the `selectedIndex` is equal to –1. The following statement says, "If the selected index is –1, we know that the text was input by the user. Otherwise, they must have chosen something that was already in the list."

```
if (findObject("theSelectName").selectedIndex == -1) {
    retVal= findObject("theSelectName").editText;
}
else {
  retVal= findObject("theSelectName").options[ findObject("theSelectName").
➥selectedIndex] .value;
}
```

AN OBJECT LOVE AFFAIR

An extension developer never forgets his or her first time. My first was twins—a matched set of objects to replace the `<sup>` and `<sub>` tags missing from Dreamweaver. I was really enamored of objects during that time and picked up some pointers I'm more than willing to pass on to you. First, let me just recommend that for any tag or code that does not require a user interface you use snippets rather than objects. What, has he completely spurned his first love? No, it's just that objects require a bit of coding and snippets are, as we used to say down south, dirt simple. When you do begin to build your objects, remember that you have to place all objects in a folder within the Configuration/Objects folder; you can use one of the existing folders or create your own. Moreover, the folder structure can go only one level deep. Unlike with custom behaviors, you can't create submenu items by nesting folders. Finally, if you're really interested in working with objects, take apart a number of the objects included in Dreamweaver. There are many excellent examples of everything from the most basic to exceedingly advanced objects.

JOLLY GOOD SHOW, INSPECTOR

What's the hardest type of extension to design? Although server behaviors are obviously quite complex code-wise, they can't touch the sheer difficulty of creating a Property inspector interface. The key to creating a Property inspector is layers—lots and lots of layers, placed very precisely. Every element, from the logo on the left to the help button on the right, is placed in a layer. When I'm building an inspector, I make extensive use of a grid (View > Grid) set to 10 pixels or less. Depending on the complexity of the inspector, you may find that you would benefit from using nested or child layers. Unlike some browsers, child layers are completely supported within Dreamweaver's rendering engine, so use as many levels as you like. Again, be sure to check the available Property inspectors within Dreamweaver to see how it's done. Don't go looking for the standard text or table inspectors, however; those are built-in to Dreamweaver and are not available as separate files.

  CHECK THIS OUT AT THE LIBRARY

Although the Tag Library Editor
is wonderful for tweaking your
code, it really begins to shine in
its ability to accept custom tags.
Choose Edit > Tag Libraries to
see all the current tags and
make their settings available for
modification. You could truly
spend days here getting your
code just the way you want it.
To add a tag, select its language
(or insert your own) and choose
Add (+). After you define a tag,
you can add attributes to it. Now,
if you really want to see some
power, how would you like to

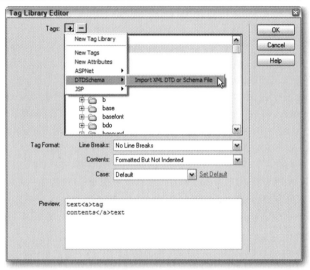

add a whole slate of tags and attributes at once? You can do exactly that if you have, at
hand or online, a DTD or schema for the language. For example, I was able to add all of
the tags and attributes for SMIL (Synchronized Multimedia Integration Language) by
downloading the files from the W3C site. Total operation time: about 23 seconds.

   TO RELOAD OR TO RESTART, THAT IS THE QUESTION…

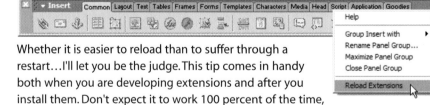

Whether it is easier to reload than to suffer through a
restart…I'll let you be the judge. This tip comes in handy
both when you are developing extensions and after you
install them. Don't expect it to work 100 percent of the time,
but it does the job for most objects and commands—at least *most* of the time. The Reload
Extensions option appears only if you Ctrl+click (Option+click) the Insert bar's Options
menu. Use the Reload Extensions trick whenever you install an object and the Extension
Manager tells you that you have to restart Dreamweaver. If the object appears, great; but
if it doesn't—usually because the object is in a new category—you'll have to restart. You
also can use this trick when writing object extensions after you save a change made to
a file so that you don't have to restart to see the update.

FRESH RIPE COMMANDS READY FOR PICKIN'

I was first introduced to this trick by one of the best extension developers around, Massimo Foti. When developing commands, you'll be doing a lot of testing along the way and you will need to save often. Unless you refresh the Commands menu, the changes since the previous save will not be visible when you go to test the command. There is an easy way to refresh the commands list without having to restart Dreamweaver or wait for extensions to reload (covered in the previous tip). Select Commands > Edit Command List and when the dialog appears, just click the Close button. Now the command is fresh and ready for you to pick so that you can get a taste of whether it works the way you expect.

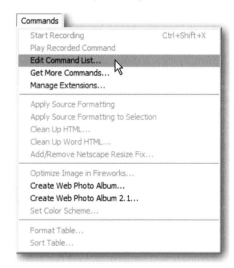

 TIME OUT FOR FLOATERS

Floaters. Sounds like jargon that might show up in a bad detective novel. In the hard-boiled Dreamweaver world, floaters are another type of extension. Now known as *panels*, floaters are so called because originally they floated above the interface and, unlike commands, stayed open and available while the page was being modified; Neil Clark's Flash Expressions panel, available from the

Dreamweaver Exchange, is a good example of a custom floater. Floaters are capable of keeping track of selections and edits to the page via two built-in functions, `selectionChanged()` and `documentEdited()`. As you might imagine, however, both are processor-intensive activities and they need to be implemented with care. It's best to include a `setTimeout()` function to slightly delay processing so that Dreamweaver doesn't freeze up. (Check out Help > Extending Dreamweaver for more info on the `setTimeout()` function and floaters.)

One other aspect to watch out for when developing custom floaters: be careful not to use a reserved name. Here's a list of names to avoid: *assets, behaviors, bindings, codesnippet, CSS styles, dataSource, documenttype, frames, helpbook, HTML styles, HTML, insertbar, launcher, layers, library, objects* or *history properties, reference, samplecontent, serverBehavior, serverFormat, serverModel, site, site files, site map, taglibrary, templates, timelines,* or *toolbar.*

THE RIGHT SIZE FOR THE RIGHT JOB

When I'm developing extensions, one of the first things I do is change Dreamweaver's default font. Dreamweaver displays its dialogs with a sans-serif font in a relatively small size; I normally create websites using a serif font and the default size. By altering the font type and size, I can better approximate how the final dialog will appear. Although this is helpful in certain exten- sions, like commands, it is absolutely critical in others, such as inspec- tors. To change the font,

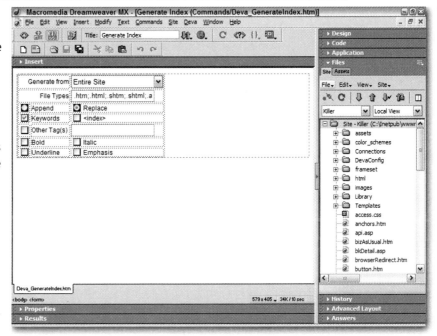

open Preferences and navigate to the Fonts category. Change the proportional font to a sans-serif one, such as Arial or Verdana. Next, drop the size down to 9 points. If we're talking style, you ask, why don't you use CSS? I avoid styling my dialogs because I want to be consistent with the "house style" and rather than second-guess it, I let Dreamweaver do the work for me.

 WHERE DOES HE GET THOSE FABULOUS TOYS?

A good 90 percent of creating a user interface for a Dreamweaver extension is made up of form elements: text fields, drop down lists, radio buttons, and check boxes, among a few others. Interspersed in the interfaces are occasional graphics, such as the folder icon typically used to open the Select File dialog. Unless you're building a completely different interface and avoiding all visual references to the Dreamweaver standard, it's less jarring to the user to retain the visual clues that are seen throughout the program. So should you go around taking snapshots of the standard Dreamweaver user interfaces and cut 'em up in a graphics program? Put down that cropping tool immediately! The kind folks from

Dreamweaverland have done the work for you; you just need to know where to look. Most of the standard images—the folder icon, lightning bolt, and up and down arrows— are stored in the Dreamweaver MX/Configuration/Shared folder in one of two folders: Shared/MM/Images or Shared/UltraDev/Images. Still can't find the image you know you've seen? Create a new site and point to the Dreamweaver MX/Configuration folder as the local site root. Then, check the Images category of the Assets panel. All the graphics used throughout Dreamweaver (even some hidden Easter Eggs) are there.

STRIP TEASER

Nearly every web developer I know has inherited a site made by someone who was a `<font>` tag fanatic. For some people, this task would be cruel and unusual punishment; but for you, it is easy.

Before starting any Find and Replace operation, I always recommend that you back up the page(s) that will be affected. Open a page that has some `<font>` tags, and then select Edit > Find and Replace or use the Ctrl+F (Command+F) keyboard shortcut. In the Search For drop-down list, choose Specific Tag. In the adjacent field, select or type **font**. You can use the Add (+) button to add parameters to the search if you'd like, but for this simple demo, let's click the Remove (–) button and not worry about using parameters. Now select Strip Tag in the Action drop-down list and proceed with finding and replacing by using the buttons on the right as you normally would. You may have caught a glimpse of other options in the Action drop-down list, including Remove Attribute, and Remove Tag & Contents. This example is only a teaser of what you can do with Find and Replace. If I know that I'll be making similar queries, I save the first one by pressing the Save Query icon (the one that looks like a disk). I save the .dwr file in a safe place and load it with the Load Query icon (the one that looks like a folder) and modify it as needed. This saves a lot of setup time—especially for complicated search patterns. With a little practice, you will save yourself loads of time with Find and Replace.

TOO MANY ITEMS ON THE MENU TO CHOOSE

Whenever I go to a restaurant that offers too many items on the menu, I have a difficult time finding what I want. I feel the same way when I've got too many items listed in my Insert menu. Nearly all of the objects in the Insert bar can be found in the Insert menu and by the time you add more objects via extensions or your own creations, the list can get so long that it actually scrolls. You can shorten the list by removing the items you don't want. To do this, look through the Macromedia\Dreamweaver MX\Configuration\Objects subfolders to find the .htm file for the object you don't want showing in the menu any more. Then open the file in Dreamweaver and add this code as the first line in the file:

```
<!-- MENU-LOCATION=NONE -->
```

Save the document and then restart Dreamweaver, or use the "To Reload or Restart, That is the Question…" tip found earlier in this chapter. You can do the same thing for the Commands menu as well if you'd like. Just locate the file in Macromedia\Dreamweaver MX\Configuration\Commands. Now you can keep your menus neat and tidy, just the way you want them.

```
1  <!-- MENU-LOCATION=NONE -->
2  <html>
3  <head>
4  <!-- Copyright 2001 Macromedia, Inc. All rights reserved. -->
5  <title>Named Anchor</title>
```

MULTI-USERS EQUALS MULTIPLE FILES

The new support for multi-user configurations is great, but it is a nightmare for extension developers as they are writing and testing their extensions. Dreamweaver first checks the user's Configuration folder for files and then looks in its own Configuration folder. The

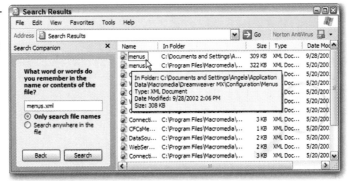

user's files takes precedence over those in the main Dreamweaver MX Configuration folder. The first thing I advise is setting up your operating system to always show hidden files. Secondly, I suggest that you use your operating system's Search feature to find files. If the results show that the same file you are looking for can be found in the user's Configuration folder and in the Dreamweaver MX Configuration folder, you'll know that you may need to edit one or both files. I've made shortcuts to both my user and Dreamweaver MX configuration folders so that I don't waste time browsing to them. I wish I could give you more specifics, but there are way too many possible scenarios. Check your operating system's help files for more information about showing hidden files and using its search interface.

    BEHIND THE SCENES OF THE HISTORY PANEL

Many times when I'm working on an extension, I know there is an API call that does what I need, but I don't remember off the top of my head what it is. Digging through the extensibility documentation is one way to find out, but I've found that if I go behind the scenes of the History panel, I often can find what I am looking for. Let me show you what I mean. Open any document and make a few changes to it in Design view so that there are several steps listed in the History panel. Now go ahead and Ctrl+Shift+click (Command+Shift+click) anywhere inside the History panel. Did you see that? Do it a few times, it is fun…You'll see the JavaScript that Dreamweaver used to execute each step. Go ahead and right-click (Ctrl+click) on a step and select Copy Steps from the context menu. If you try to paste in any open file in Dreamweaver, it will likely just execute the step as though you'd pressed the Replay button. Instead, paste to a plain text file outside of Dreamweaver to view the code. This is a really great way to learn about Dreamweaver Extension API and see how Dreamweaver does its thing.

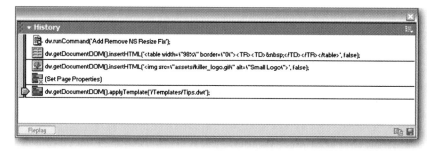

MAKING YOUR OWN NEW FROM TEMPLATE COMMAND

As promised in the tip "Whatever Happened to New from Template?" in Chapter 6, here's how you'll be able to make your very own New from Template command:

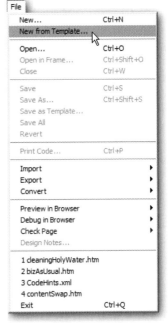

(1) Follow the tip "Multi-Users Equals Multiple Files" earlier in this chapter to locate the menus.xml file. Back up and store the file in a safe place in case you need it later.

(2) Now open the original menus.xml file in Dreamweaver. Next, use Find to locate DWMenu_File, which should bring you close to line number 1605. This is the code from which the File menu is created.

(3) Below the first `<menuitem>` tag, type the following tag:

```
<menuitem
name=" New from Template..."
enabled=n" true"
command=" dw.newFromTemplate();"
domrequired=" false"
id=" YOURNAME_File_New_From_Template" />
```

Be sure to change *YOURNAME* to your own name or some other unique identifier. As a special touch, you could add a `<separator />` after the `<menuitem>` tag you added to make a horizontal rule below the menu item.

(4) Save the document.

(5) Restart Dreamweaver.

Now when you look under the File menu, you should see New from Template as an option. Pretty simple, isn't it?

     REORGANIZING THE INSERT BAR

Go ahead and try as hard as you can to move the tabs that make up the categories of the Insert bar. Sorry, you just can't do that. You can't use the Group With submenu of the Options menu to group the tabs with other panels, either. That's just a fact of life. You can change the order of the categories, however, by altering the Insertbar.xml file found in your user configuration's Objects folder. (See "Multi-Users Equals Multiple Files" earlier in this chapter for more detail.) If you've never added custom objects, you won't find the Insertbar.xml file in your user configuration's Objects folder. You'll have to modify the Insertbar.xml file in the Dreamweaver MX\Configuration\Objects folder instead, or create a folder named Objects and add a copy if Insertbar.xml to it in your user configuration.

Make a backup of the Insertbar.xml file before you make any changes, just in case. When you open the file you should notice that each `<category>` tag contains `<button>` tags. Move a category by moving it and all its contents before or after another `<category>` tag. You can identify which Insert bar category is represented by the value of the `id` attribute (with the exception of the Layout category, which has a value of `tools`). The order in which the categories appear in the file when you save it will be the order in which they appear in the Insert bar when you restart Dreamweaver. How good are you at alphabetizing?

MY DOCUMENTS

You have a slew of document file types to choose from in New Document dialog, and they each have their very own default document in the configuration that can be customized to suit your needs. Dynamic pages such as .asp and .cfm files do not contain a default `doctype`, like this one used in the default .htm file:

```
<!DOCTYPE HTML PUBLIC "-//W3C//DTD HTML 4.01 Transitional//EN">
```

You can add this or whatever else you want to the appropriate default file located in the Macromedia\Dreamweaver MX\Configuration\DocumentTypes\NewDocuments folder.

After you edit the file, save it and open a new file of its kind in Dreamweaver to verify that all your changes are what you expect. Customizing the documents to include things common to all pages you develop—such as copyright notices and `doctype`—ensures that you never forget to include the information and saves you all the time it would have taken to add the code for each new page.

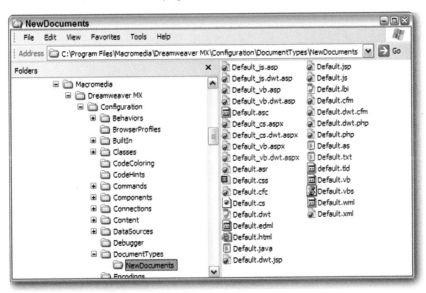

OBJECT TO RUN A COMMAND

You've made a History command or maybe even a command of your very own, but wouldn't it be nice if it could have its own little icon on the Insert bar? All you need to know is the filename of the command and you can make an object that calls a command. Here are the steps:

(1) Open the Insertbar.xml file found in your user configuration's Objects folder. (See "Multi-Users Equals Multiple Files" earlier in this chapter for more detail.)

(2) Locate the category where you want the new object to appear.

(3) Add this code and be sure to change each attribute's placeholder value appropriately:

```
<button
command="dw.runCommand('My Command File Name Here.htm',null);"
enabled=""
id="SomethingTotallyUnique"
image="theCategory\ MyImageName.gif"
name="This Is The Tool Tip Text For The Object" />
```

An example of a button that calls the Apply Source Formatting command is shown here:

```
<button
command="dw.runCommand('Apply Source Formatting.htm',null);"
enabled=""
id="killerTips_ApplySourceFomatting"
image="Common\ sourceFormat.gif"
name="Apply Source Formatting" />
```

A unique id is required and you'll need an 18×18 pixel image stored in the location specified by the image attribute.

(4) Save the Insertbar.xml file and then restart Dreamweaver.

PICK AN OBJECT, ANY OBJECT

Whenever you write an extension that requires input from the user, you've got to have a form with at least one field. To get the value of the field, you first need to be able to find it. The old-fashioned way is to use `document.theFormName.theFieldName.value`. If you add a link to the UI.js file (located in Macromedia\Dreamweaver MX\Configuration\ Shared\MM\ Scripts\CMN\), you can take advantage of Macromedia's `findObject()` function. A link to the JavaScript file would look similar to the following code:

```
<script language="JavaScript"
src="../../Shared/MM/Scripts/CMN/UI.js"></script>
```

Now let's say you have a text field named theUsername. Instead of using the following line:

```
var myUsername = document.theForm.theUsername.value
```

you would use:

```
var myUsername = findObject("theUsername").value
```

Use `findObject` if you're concerned with supporting earlier versions of Dreamweaver. If Dreamweaver MX is all that matters to you, use `dwscripts.findDOMObject()` instead and be sure to include the link to dwscripts.js found in Macromedia\Dreamweaver MX\Configuration\Shared\Common\Scripts.

Not only is this code shorter, but it is fast, efficient, and lessens your chance of typos.

   ## RATED X: MACROMEDIA CODE EXPOSED

This tip is rated X for eXtremely sophisticated. If you feel the urge to change an existing Macromedia server behavior, you'll either need to make copies of all involved files and hand-code the changes, or try

to do it through the Server Behavior Builder. In order to get the server behavior to appear in the New Server Behavior dialog, you must first modify its .edml file. Find the original server behavior's .edml file in the appropriate server model folder under Macromedia\ Dreamweaver MX\Configuration\ServerBehaviors\. You're looking for the .edml file that contains `hideFromBuilder="true"`. Change the `true` to `false`, save the file, and then restart Dreamweaver. Now click the Server Behavior panel's Add (+) button and then select New Server Behavior from the drop-down list. Yes, I noticed there was Edit Server Behavior Option. Don't use it on Macromedia's server behaviors! It is safer to copy an existing server behavior and just have your own version of it than to risk ruining the original server behavior.

INDEX

modifying. *See* changing

mouse
making selections, 181
selecting rows and
columns, 48

mouse movements, 197

**Move To Record server
behaviors, 159**

**Move To Specific Record
behavior, 170**

moving
cells, 64
content in tables, 65
from document to document, 5
items in head tags, 176
layers, 99
rulers, 10
tables from Excel to
Dreamweaver, 54

multiple selection, 173

N

named anchors, 144

naming
floaters, names to avoid, 210
frames, 108
framesets, 106
radio buttons, 142
template regions, 115

naming conventions, 140
dynamic sites, 155

navigation, recordsets
hiding, 162
Recordset Navigation Bar, 168

Navigation Bar object, 128

navigation bars, creating, 128

**nested framesets,
changing, 107**

nesting
layers, 103
tables, 59

Netscape 4.x
margins, 80
parentheses, 80
placing images in backgrounds
of tables, 81
resizing layers, 100

**Netscape Gecko engine,
AOL, 78**

Netscape Resize Fix, 100

New From Template, 126, 217

noscript tags, 145

null links, # (octothorpes), 135

numbers, aligning decimals, 52

O

object dialogs, bypassing, 17

objects, 207
click-and-drag objects, 177
creating
for commands, 220
the recordset for the
master page, 169
Date, 130
Email Link, 145
finding with findObject()
function, 221
Flash Text, 131
Navigation Bar, 128

octothorpes (#), 135

opening browser windows, 89

orientation of Insert bar, 10

**origins of rulers, returning
to, 10**

overlapping layers, 102

P

pages
clearing, 136
master-detail pages, 169
updating, 118

Panel groups
docking, 4
expanding to maximum
height, 16

panels
arranging in workspace, 4
Assets, sharing assets, 12
floating panels, finding lost
panels, 6
hiding, 9
HomeSite Coder, 4
icons, Launcher, 8
removing, 21
shortcuts, 20
Snippet, 36, 180
Validation, 189

**paragraphs, copying from Word
into Dreamweaver, 134**

parentheses, browsers, 80

Paste HTML command, 65

paths
CSS, 28
document relative paths, 28
to graphics, 141
root relative paths, 28

**pixel-perfect positioning,
layers, 101**

placement of Design view, 13

point-to-file, 24

pointers, hand pointers, 38

popup windows, closing, 77
closing and returning to the
top of the page, 135

positioning
layers, pixel-perfect
positioning, 101
text between graphics, 138

**POST method, Live Data
view, 169**

pre-filled forms, 152

pre-selected values, 148

www.informit.com

YOUR GUIDE TO IT REFERENCE

New Riders has partnered with **InformIT.com** to bring technical information to your desktop. Drawing from New Riders authors and reviewers to provide additional information on topics of interest to you, **InformIT.com** provides free, in-depth information you won't find anywhere else.

Articles

Keep your edge with thousands of free articles, in-depth features, interviews, and IT reference recommendations— all written by experts you know and trust.

Online Books

Answers in an instant from **InformIT Online Books'** 600+ fully searchable online books.

POWERED BY

Catalog

Review online sample chapters, author biographies, and customer rankings and choose exactly the right book from a selection of over 5,000 titles.

www.newriders.com

VISIT OUR WEB SITE

WWW.NEWRIDERS.COM

On our Web site you'll find information about our other books, authors, tables of contents, indexes, and book errata. You will also find information about book registration and how to purchase our books.

EMAIL US

Contact us at this address: **nrfeedback@newriders.com**

- If you have comments or questions about this book
- To report errors that you have found in this book
- If you have a book proposal to submit or are interested in writing for New Riders
- If you would like to have an author kit sent to you
- If you are an expert in a computer topic or technology and are interested in being a technical editor who reviews manuscripts for technical accuracy
- To find a distributor in your area, please contact our international department at this address. **nrmedia@newriders.com**

- For instructors from educational institutions who want to preview New Riders books for classroom use. Email should include your name, title, school, department, address, phone number, office days/hours, text in use, and enrollment, along with your request for desk/examination copies and/or additional information.
- For members of the media who are interested in reviewing copies of New Riders books. Send your name, mailing address, and email address, along with the name of the publication or Web site you work for.

BULK PURCHASES/CORPORATE SALES

The publisher offers discounts on this book when ordered in quantity for bulk purchases and special sales. For sales within the U.S., please contact: Corporate and Government Sales (800) 382-3419 or **corpsales@pearsontechgroup.com**. Outside of the U.S., please contact: International Sales (317) 581-3793 or **international@pearsontechgroup.com**.

WRITE TO US

New Riders Publishing
201 W. 103rd St.
Indianapolis, IN 46290-1097

CALL US

Toll-free (800) 571-5840 + 9 + 7477
If outside U.S. (317) 581-3500. Ask for New Riders.

FAX US

(317) 581-4663

New Riders